WORLD'S BEST OUTDOOR GAMES

Written and Illustrated by
Glen Vecchione

Sterling Publishing Co., Inc.   New York

To my brother Josh,
for all the fun we had playing outdoors

Library of Congress Cataloging-in-Publication Data

Vecchione, Glen.
   World's best outdoor games / written and illustrated by Glen
Vecchione.
      p.   cm.
   Includes index.
   Summary: Presents a variety of games meant to be played outside
—in such settings as yards, fields, playgrounds, and beaches—giving
suitable ages, number of players, and space requirements for each
game.
   ISBN 0-8069-8436-8
   1. Games—Juvenile literature.   2. Outdoor recreation—Juvenile
literature. [1. Games. 2. Outdoor recreations.] I. Title.
GV1203.V384   1992
790.1—dc20   92-19101
                                                           CIP
                                                           AC

10 9 8 7 6 5 4 3 2 1

Published in 1992 by Sterling Publishing Company, Inc.
387 Park Avenue South, New York, N.Y. 10016
© 1992 by Glen Vecchione
Distributed in Canada by Sterling Publishing
% Canadian Manda Group, P.O. Box 920, Station U
Toronto, Ontario, Canada M8Z 5P9
Distributed in Great Britain and Europe by Cassell PLC
Villiers House, 41/47 Strand, London WC2N 5JE, England
Distributed in Australia by Capricorn Link Ltd.
P.O. Box 665, Lane Cove, NSW 2066
Manufactured in the United States of America
All rights reserved

Sterling ISBN 0-8069-8436-8

Contents

Before You Begin

Turn off the video game, put away your Walkman, get up from your computer and *come out to play*! We've collected some of the best, the most unusual, the *just darned greatest* outdoor games in the world.

These games emphasize physical prowess and grace of movement, as well as team spirit and individual initiative.

There's something special here for every player: Thinkers will enjoy strategy games like "Capture the Flag" or "Chain Gang Race"; creative players will lose themselves in "Streamer Ball" or "Throwing Tops"; and everyone else will just have to settle for a plain good time!

All the games challenge and entertain without being hurtful physically or emotionally. You can play most of them with mixed groups of girls and boys from age 8 up, and adults appreciate almost every one. We've included a few games for younger children, too—so if in doubt about any game, check the age range chart in the back of the book.

We've also listed specific requirements for each game right at the start, so that you can see at a glance the space you need and how many people. And what variety you'll find—games for fields and front porches, picnics and backyard barbeques; games familiar and some, frankly, strange.

A word of caution: If we suggest a paved surface for a particular game, avoid the street and find a schoolyard or gym instead. The streets of today hardly resemble the streets of days gone by when fewer cars rattled the calm of a neighborhood on lazy summer afternoons.

In many parts of the country developers and urban planners have introduced "play streets"—closed streets and intersections having all the authenticity of the real thing, except for cars. Some of our games work well in this setting.

And so, we present the *World's Best Outdoor Games*. Put on your old play clothes and—ENJOY!

1
Fabulous Flying Frisbees

Everyone loves tossing a Frisbee! Whether at the beach or in the park, a Frisbee volley between two, three, four, or 20 people is great exercise. It's also fun just watching the disc as it soars back and forth over the heads of the running players!

The games in this chapter require nothing more than the simple skill of tossing the Frisbee backhand—the most basic throw.

FRISBEE HISTORY

According to popular legend, the first Frisbees were metal pie tins tossed around the campus by Yale students in the early 1920's. The source? The Frisbie Pie Company of Bridgeport, Connecticut.

The wobbling tins skittered across colleges, beaches and city streets until the mid-1940's when a West Coast inventor named Fred Morrison had a better idea. Plastic was the ideal stuff for Morrison's new design, and soon the granddaddy of the modern Frisbee was born—an unwieldy disc of "radio plastic" that shattered if it hit the ground too hard!

After a few more experiments, Morrison discovered the injection mold and a softer material: polyethylene. The modern Frisbee—or "Pluto Platter" as it was then called—was born, making its debut at the Pomona County Fair in Los Angeles. Hundreds of "Pluto Platters" were sold before a small toy company looking for a hot new item approached Morrison in 1955. Soon Wham-O Toys was producing thousands of the flying discs and renaming them "Frisbees"—an unintentional misspelling of the original Frisbie Pie Company name.

More Frisbees are sold in one year than all the baseballs, footballs and basketballs combined!

HOW TO THROW AND CATCH A FRISBEE

For the backhand throw, slip the edge of the Frisbee into the space between your thumb and first finger. Your thumb is on top, your other fingers fan out beneath the disc for a firm (but not too tight) grip.

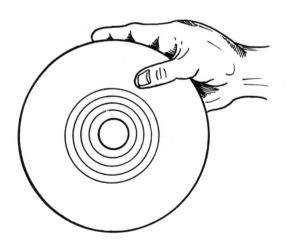

Stand sideways with your throwing side towards the target. Curl your throwing arm in towards your chest, then whip it outward, giving the Frisbee an extra snap with your wrist.

To catch the Frisbee, you can use either the thumbs-up or thumbs-down technique. Either method works well for a fairly relaxed volley between players.

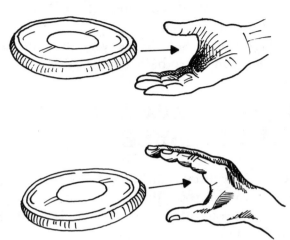

Of course, when you're playing hard, *anything goes*—a Frisbee clapped between both hands for a jump-catch, landing pizza-pie style on your palm, or nabbed between your knees—is all fair game!

Guts

Players:	**10 (5 to a team)**
Materials:	**Frisbee**
	Chalk or rope to mark boundaries
Surface:	**Paved or grassy**

Guts is the great-granddaddy of all Frisbee games. It was first played with cookie tin lids on the campus of

Dartmouth College in the later 1920's. It's simple enough to learn in a matter of minutes and challenging enough to keep you amused for hours!

The field is 15 yards long by 10 yards wide (13.5m × 9m), or approximately the width of five players with arms outstretched. Since no jumping is allowed, the upper limit for an in-bounds throw is the height of the upstretched arms of the players. Catches can be made at any distance behind the goal line.

The object is to throw the Frisbee through your opponents' goal space without their catching it. This is easier said than done since, as in volleyball, your opponents will back each other up in order to nab the disc as it sails through the air—that is, if it *does* sail through the air!

There are several trick throws that can keep your opponents hopping (remember, no jumping!) such as:

- **The Grounder:** Thrown at a 45° angle hard against the ground so that the Frisbee ricochets up at about the same angle and heads straight for the kneecaps of your opponents.

- **The Turnover:** A flip-of-the-wrist throw that causes the disc to fly vertically towards your opponents. It's like catching a saw blade.

- **The Upside-downer:** Tossing a Frisbee upside down causes some unpredictable behavior in flight. Dips, curves and sudden skyward leaps are not unheard of with this technique.

Of course, teams may decide to outlaw any or all of these throws depending on the level of difficulty desired.

SCORING

Claim one point for each throw your opponents miss. They receive a point if your throw is out of bounds in any of the following ways: sailing above the height of their out-stretched arms, landing outside the lateral bounds of the field, or dropping to the ground in front of their goal (perhaps an unsuccessful "grounder").

After the two teams are chosen, the game begins with a flip of the coin to determine which team will serve first. Any member of the serving team may start the volley, which continues until someone misses a catch or tosses the Frisbee out-of-bounds. Then, the servers become the receivers or vice versa.

The first team to rack up 21 points wins.

Goal Line Frisbee

Players:	**6–20 (3–10 on a team)**
Materials:	**Frisbee**
	Rope or wooden stakes for marking boundaries
Surface:	**Grassy**

This uncomplicated toss-for-the-goal Frisbee game is still one of the most appealing both to play and to watch. The playing field can be as small or as large as you'd like, according to the age and expertise of the players. Mark goal lines clearly at the ends of the playing field, but you can simply rough out the width by stakes, ropes or natural landmarks.

The object of the game is to throw the Frisbee over the opposing team's goal line for a point. Any and all throwing techniques are allowed, even rolling the Frisbee along the ground hula-hoop style for a surprise assault!

Players from each team toss a coin to determine which team will make the initial throw and which team will defend the goal. The throwing team takes an advantageous position distance-wise for the first throw—five feet (1.5m) in front of their goal line (shorten this distance if the playing field is shorter). If the defending team catches the throw, the catcher may take five running steps in any direction—a "reward" since running with the Frisbee is forbidden. Otherwise, the throw is returned from wherever the Frisbee lands until one of the teams scores.

The game is won either by a point score (21 points) or by limiting the playing time to one hour.

Double Disc Frisbee _____

Players: **2 + a referee**
Materials: **2 identical Frisbees**
               Rope and four wooden stakes for marking boundaries
Surface: **Grassy**

This game calls for a keen eye and fast legs—two discs sail through the air at the same time as players try to score by dropping discs in the opposing goal area without touching boundary lines or foul barriers.

The playing court is divided into three sections: two goal areas at the sides—12 feet × 14 feet each (3.6m × 4.2m)—and one common area in the center—14 feet × 20 feet (4.2m × 6m). Goal and playing areas are further separated by two narrow foul barriers—2 inches × 2 inches × 14 feet (5cm × 5cm × 4.2m)—marked off with wooden stakes.

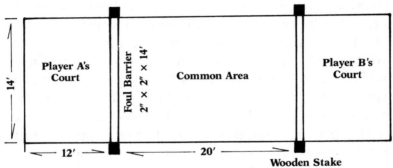

Each player stands in his area and attempts to score a goal by tossing his Frisbee over the center and landing it in his opponent's area. At the same time, each player is defending his area from his opponent's throw.

Play begins with a signal from a referee who will also keep track of points and halt the play after someone scores. A disc that lands within the boundaries of the opposing goal area scores one point for the thrower. A disc that is thrown out-of-bounds or is caught scores one point for the receiver.

An interesting twist is that often one player winds up either throwing or catching both discs as the players move in and out of "phase" with each other. But a sharp-eyed referee will make sure the scoring is fair and accurate—21 points for the win.

Courtsbee

Players: 2
Materials: Frisbee
Chalk for marking court boundaries
Four poles, trash cans, or any other standing
objects to mark boundaries
Surface: Paved

The trick of this game is the skip, so a hard, paved surface is required. To skip a Frisbee you throw it towards the ground forcefully at a 45° angle. The Frisbee will rebound off the pavement and climb again! Don't worry if you don't get it right the first time—practice makes perfect.

Each player occupies a 12 feet × 7 feet (3.5m × 2m) court from which they both serve and receive volleys. Between courts is a narrower area on which the Frisbee is skipped, marked off by goalposts, measuring 20 feet × 5 feet (6m × 1.5m). This area is off-limits to both players.

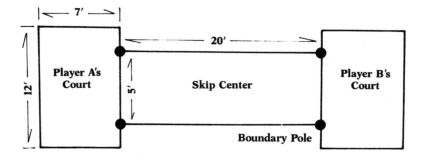

The object of the game is to accumulate 21 points for the win by skipping the Frisbee back and forth until a player misses. The thrower skips his Frisbee within the boundaries of the marked-out center area for a legal throw. The catcher returns it without stepping outside the boundaries of his court.

The volley continues until someone either misses a catch, steps outside the boundaries to make a catch, throws outside the boundaries, or fails to skip the Frisbee when throwing it. Players may throw the Frisbee as hard and fast as desired, as long as it skips within the boundaries of the center area as marked out by the four posts. A player may calculate his skip so that the Frisbee either bounces high in the air on the rebound, or hugs the ground, barely making it to the other side. Fun.

Boomerang Frisbee

Players:	2
Materials:	Frisbee
	Chalk or rope to mark boundaries
Surface:	Paved or short cropped grass

Everyone is familiar with the boomerang—that strange, flying shoehorn-of-a-thing born in Australia. The magic of the boomerang is that once it's thrown it comes right back to the thrower. Well, with a little practice for the correct angle, a Frisbee behaves in exactly the same way! This makes for a wonderful two-player game.

With chalk or rope, mark out a 10 × 15 foot (3m × 4.5m) rectangular box. Both players stand inside this box and flip a coin to decide who will be the first to throw the Frisbee.

The thrower tosses his Frisbee at a 45° angle or greater, so that it begins to boomerang and fall back towards him. At this point the catcher must intercept the Frisbee before it hits the ground. If he catches it, he tosses it (or boomerangs it) in the air again for his opponent to catch.

This continues with neither player leaving the box until someone scores enough points to win the game. The thrower scores when the receiver misses the Frisbee or steps outside of the box to catch it. The receiver scores when the Frisbee is thrown out-of-bounds—that is, if it boomerangs back to a point clearly outside the confines of the rectangle—or if it doesn't boomerang at *all*.

The first player to reach 21 points wins the game.

Circle Frisbee

Players: 10 (5 on a team)
Materials: Frisbee
Yardstick or rope, 15 yards (13.5m) long, marked off at each yard
Chalk for marking boundaries
Surface: Paved

This game is unusual in that it requires a circular playing field 30 yards (27m) in diameter, with a small central circle three feet (1m) in diameter for the goal. One player from the defending team stands in this circle and acts as a target. This "human goalpost" may twist around, jump, or dodge a throw, but he cannot leave the allotted space. If he catches the Frisbee, he may throw it back out to one of his teammates. In that case, the sides reverse and the thrower from the opposing team becomes the new goal-post.

Toss a coin to decide which team defends and which team scores. The player who is the goalpost takes his position and begins the game by throwing the Frisbee to one of his teammates. As in the scrimmage of a basketball game, both teams scramble for possession of the Frisbee. The team whose member is the goalpost will try to prevent the Frisbee from hitting the goal by intercepting a throw from its opponents and then tossing it among themselves. Or, a player may assist in defending his team's goal by jumping and blocking the Frisbee so that it falls to the ground. Of course, the opposing team formulates whatever throwing strategy is needed to hit the goal.

Circle Frisbee requires frequent changing of sides as the Frisbee is dropped, missed or intercepted by the opposing team. When this occurs, the player of the fumbling team who's closest to the center becomes the new goalpost. The Frisbee may be walked, but only backwards.

Goal points are accumulated according to the distance of the successful throw. For instance, a player who hits the goalpost at 15 yards (13.5m) is awarded 15 points while a player who hits at 10 yards (9m) is awarded only 10 points. Measure distance by using the yardstick or by stretching the measured rope from the goalpost to the thrower. Throws of less than five yards (4.5m) count for no points.

The first team to reach 21 points wins the game.

Street Frisbee ————————————————

Players: 4–10 (2–5 on a team)
Materials: Frisbee
         Chalk for marking boundaries
Surface: Street with curbs

This game, invented by Dr. Stancil Johnson of Pennsylvania, is a kind of variation on two familiar ballgames:

"Keep-away" and "Dodge." There are usually three or four players to a team—more players can become unwieldy in the street.

The unusual feature of this game is that the Frisbee is deliberately kept low—barely off the ground—to take advantage of the curbs for ricochet shots. Draw goal lines 10 to 15 yards (.9m–13.5m) apart. There is no backward limit to the goal area.

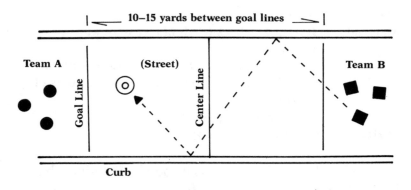

The object of the game is to toss the Frisbee so that it comes to a dead stop behind your opponent's goal line, without him or his teammates catching it. Fumbles, or stomping a skittering disc to keep it still, count as points for the thrower.

Flip a coin to decide which team serves first. The server—anyone on the serving team—throws the Frisbee at his opponents, keeping it low enough to bounce off the curb in unpredictable directions. It can be pretty funny watching your opponents scramble to catch a shot, the direction of which they haven't figured out yet!

If the Frisbee lands behind the goal line, it counts as a point for the throwers. If the opposing team catches the Frisbee—even from behind the goal line—they return it in the same way. The volley continues until one team either scores a point, or fumbles the Frisbee by dropping it or throwing it out-of-bounds. The scoring team serves again. The fumbling team surrenders the serve to its opponents.

The first team to score 21 points wins the game.

Frisbee Bowling

Players: 2–10
Materials: Several Frisbees (each player may want to use his own)
10 mailing tubes, 2 to 3 feet (.6m × 1m) long
Modelling clay to weigh down the bottoms of the tubes
Chalk or rope to mark boundaries
Surface: Paved or short cropped grass

Frisbee bowling isn't as easy as it sounds. Imagine a bowling ball that not only weaves from side to side, but dips and wobbles and curves in the air. Now there's a trick!

Arrange the "pins" (the mailing tubes) just as in a regular game of bowling. The "alley" length and scoring method are the same, too. Try experimenting with different weights for the pins if you want a more or less challenging game. No doubt you'll come up with some fancy "throws" as well. Remember, a "gutter Frisbee" is a shot that sails out and away from your pins and lands in your neighbor's flowerbed!

Ultimate Frisbee

Players: 11–25 (5–12 on a team) + a referee
Materials: Frisbee
                 Chalk or rope for marking boundaries
Surface: Paved or grassy

The object of this football-like Frisbee game is to gain points by scoring goals. A goal is scored when a player successfully throws the Frisbee to a teammate standing beyond the goal line of the opposing team. Teams switch sides after each goal.

Mark out a playing field 60 yards (54m) long with 40 yard-wide (36m) goal lines. Lateral boundaries are not absolutely necessary. As in "Guts" and "Street Frisbee," there are no limits behind the goal areas.

Both teams stand behind their respective goal lines until the opening throw (from a member of either team—toss a coin for it). Then, the receiving team either catches the toss or allows the Frisbee to land and runs to retrieve it. Once the Frisbee is picked up, it may be passed by throwing it from player to player *only*. No running is allowed from that point on, except for the few balancing steps a player may take after catching or intercepting a "pass."

Since opposing players attempt to wrestle the Frisbee away from one another after it's thrown, a good strategy for passing and guarding is advisable. For passing: Teammates might agree to duck and throw the Frisbee low to the ground. For guarding: They might stand in a loose circle around the player who has the Frisbee.

Also advisable is a firm agreement between teams on what constitutes foul play—touching an opponent as you grab for his Frisbee might be fine, but holding him down in order to wrestle it from him should not be allowed.

When a goal is scored, the referee calls it out and halts the game—this is a perfect time for each team to "huddle" and formulate a new plan. The scoring team makes the next opening throw.

Ultimate Frisbee is timed to determine the winner—two 24-minute halves with a 10-minute half-time. As in football, the last few minutes can be a real hair-raiser!

2
Ridiculous Relays & Other Races

The idea of a relay race probably started in ancient times, when a messenger ran for miles over hills and fields to the point of exhaustion. Luckily, a second messenger was waiting to take over, and a third messenger after him, and so the good or bad news travelled—was *relayed*—from messenger to messenger across the countryside.

Relay races are fun because they can involve a large number of players, each one alternating race time with rest time so that no one gets too tired. Relay races also encourage and develop "team spirit"—for however fast an individual racer might be, it's the *team* that actually wins or loses the game.

Sleeping Bag Relay Race _____

Players: 16–30 (8–15 on a team)
Materials: 2 sleeping bags
Rope or wooden stakes for marking start and finish lines
Surface: Grassy or sandy

This is a variation on one of the simplest and most popular of picnic relay races—the burlap bag race. Sleeping bags are even more fun because they're bulky and harder to "steer." Most are also deep enough to swallow an unwary racer after the first few hops—to the delight of the competition!

Mark out start and finish lines 15 yards (13.5m) apart. You can adjust this distance for smaller players if necessary. All players remove their shoes and each team divides in half, so that there are two lines of at least four players facing each other from opposite ends of the racing field.

The first players of each team wait behind the starting line with a sleeping bag beside them on the ground. At the "Go" signal, they pick up the bags, climb in, and hop across the field to waiting teammates. Bags are handed over only after the original racers cross the finish line. The second racers hop back across to the starting line and turn the bags over to the third racers; the third racers hop back to the finish line and give their bags to the fourth racers, and so on.

The first team to have the last racer hop back across the starting line wins the game.

Wiggle Relay Race

Players: 12–20 (6–10 players on a team)
Materials: Rope for marking start and finish lines
Surface: Grassy

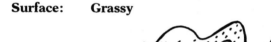

Wear old clothes for this one, because you'll be grassy-green before it's over. Stretch two lengths of rope across the ground at opposite sides of the racing field. The ropes mark the start and finish lines and each one should be about ten feet (3m) long. Or, you can use wooden stakes separated by the same distance. The racing field should be less than 12 yards (11m), because anything longer tires everybody out—remember, this is a wiggle race!

Each team divides in half and two lines of at least three players face each other from behind the start and finish lines at opposite sides of the field. At the "Go" signal, the first player of each team dives to his stomach, clasps his hands behind his back, and wiggles across the grass to the opposite side where his teammate waits. Racers may use feet and legs to push themselves forward, but their hands must remain clasped behind their backs and the wiggle proceeds on the belly only. Any violation of this rule allows the other team to call "Foul!"—which means the offending player goes back to the starting point.

When a wiggling racer reaches the other side, he tags his teammate's foot with his nose. The second wiggler dives to the ground and wiggles back across, tagging a third wiggler, and so on. The winning wiggler comes back across the field from the finish line side, tagging the first, or original wiggler.

In case you haven't figured it out yet, it's pretty hard to wiggle forward in a straight line. Half the fun of this game is watching the competing wigglers collide with each other as they get off course!

Whose Shoes?

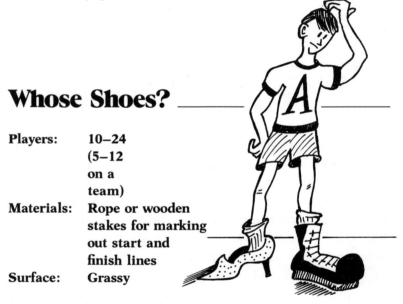

Players:	10–24 (5–12 on a team)
Materials:	Rope or wooden stakes for marking out start and finish lines
Surface:	Grassy

Ever wonder what it's like in the other person's shoes? In this relay race—perfect for that sunny day picnic—you get to find out.

Mark out start and finish lines at opposite ends of the racing field, 20 yards (18m) apart. Players of each team line up one behind the other and wait for the starting signal.

At the sound of "Go!" the first player walks as fast as possible to the finish line where he removes his shoes. He returns without shoes to the start line where he tags the second player and goes to the end of the line.

The second player walks to the finish line, removes his shoes, puts on the first player's shoes (without lacing them), and wobbles back to the start line where he tags the third player and goes to the end of the line.

The third player follows the same procedure, followed by the fourth player, then the fifth, until the last player returns from the finish line to tag the first player.

Now, the shoeless first player dashes back across to the finish line where he puts on the shoes the last player left behind, and wobbles back to the starting line, where he calls: "Whose shoes?" At this point, all players on the team sit down and switch shoes. When a player finds his own shoes and puts them on, he stands. The first team to have all players standing wins the game.

Pass-the-Grapefruit Relay _____

Players: **10–20 (5–10 on a team)**
Materials: **2 large grapefruits, cold if possible**
Surface: **Paved or grassy**

You're probably familiar with "Pass-the-Grapefruit"—the popular party game where a grapefruit is passed under the chin from player to player. In this relay race the grapefruit is carried by each racer who then passes it to his waiting teammate—all under the chin! But there's another twist at the end . . .

Mark out start and finish lines and place them 10 yards (9m) apart. Divide each team in half so that five racers line up behind the start line, and the other five line up behind the finish line. A grapefruit is placed behind the start line at the foot of each team's first racer.

At the "Go" signal, the first racer jumps down on "all-fours" and picks up the grapefruit by tucking it under his chin—no hands! He stands up with the grapefruit, clasps his hands behind his back, and runs across to the finish line where his teammate waits. If he drops his grapefruit, he must drop down on all fours to pick it up again. Behind the finish line, teammates pass the grapefruits under the chin. The first racer goes to the end of the line and the second racer runs back to the start line to pass his grapefruit to the third racer, and so on. When the last racer passes his grapefruit back to the first, or original racer, both halves of the team run from opposite sides of the field and combine to make one line, ten players long—or as many players as are on the team.

Now it's pass-the-grapefruit time. The first racer passes his grapefruit to the next in line, who passes it to the next in line. The last person in line to receive the grapefruit shouts "Time," winning the game for his team.

Dizzy Race

Players:	**4–10**
Materials:	**Blindfold**
	Chalk or rope for marking finish line
Surface:	**Paved or grassy**

Hilarious—particularly with more than four players—"Dizzy Race" provides side-splitting scenes of goofy racers colliding or walking off in the wrong direction.

Each racer has a "spotter" who guides him safely. Blindfolded, spun 10 times by the spotter, then straightened out and pointed towards the finish line 50 feet (15m) away, the racer tries to get his balance.

At the signal, racers stumble towards the finish line with their spotters close beside them. Spotters must guide their racers away from the danger of a tree, bush or lamppost, but they are not allowed to indicate in which direction to walk.

The first racer to cross the finish line wins. Racers and spotters change places for the next game.

Balloon-Face Relay

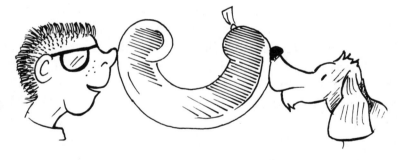

Players:	16–40 (8–20 on a team), but always an even number
Materials:	2 large balloons, partially inflated
	Chalk or rope for marking start and finish lines
Surface:	Paved or grassy

It's a good idea to have the pairs of racers on each team matched up for height—it's part of an effective winning strategy for this game.

Inflate two balloons so that each one is firm enough to hold its shape but soft enough to be carried between two faces—that's right, two *faces*. Mark out start and finish lines at opposite sides of the racing field, about 15 yards (13.5m) apart.

Each racer pairs off with another member of his own team, and each team divides in half, so that half the pairs of racers wait behind the start line, opposite the other half behind the finish line.

At the start line, one player of each pair holds a balloon at his side and waits for the "Go" signal. At the signal, he squeezes the balloon between his face and his partner's and both clasp their hands behind their backs. Then both partners start walking as fast as possible towards the finish line. Only a sideways walk is possible, and hands must remain clasped behind backs while the balloon is carried. If the balloon slips out from between the two faces, it must hit the ground before either player may unclasp his hands and pick it up. Since that usually takes enough time to slow down a pair of racers considerably, the pair does *not* have to return to the start line as a penalty.

When the first pair of racers reaches the finish line, they must cross it completely before transferring the balloon to the second pair of waiting racers. No hands are used in the switch! The second pair approaches the balloon perpendicularly from opposite sides, and maneuvers around so that the balloon is switched without being dropped.

The second pair of racers walks back to the starting line where the third pair waits, and so on. When the last pair comes back from the finish line side, they win the game for their team.

Junk Shop Relay

Players: 21–41 (10–20 on a team), but always an even number + a referee

Materials: 2 identical sets of various objects, each object small enough to pass from one player to the next

Surface: Paved or grassy

For this nerve-wracking relay race, the racers are usually still while the objects go a-flying!

The players of each team sit or stand in a row facing the opposite team. Next to the first player is a pile of objects that might include a small pillow, a coffee mug, a feather, a cowboy hat—you decide on the kind and number of things to pass. Remember, there must be two of each object, one for each team.

The referee stands between the two teams and begins the game by calling out an object, following it with a command such as: "Throw in the air and catch!" Each team's first player must search through his pile for the named object, then carry out the action before he passes the object to the next in line, who in turn repeats the action before she passes it to the next player, and so on. Some fun commands might be "Hat—put it on, make a strange face, take it off!" or "Feather—tickle the person next to you!" or "Pillow—get up, smack the player sitting opposite you, sit down again!" The referee really gets to use his imagination for this one!

After carrying out the action, the last player in line tosses the object onto the finish pile. The first team to pass all objects to the end wins the game.

Siamese Twins Relay

S T A R T

Players:	**16–40 (8–20 on a team), but always an even number**
Materials:	**Chalk or rope for marking start and finish lines**
Surface:	**Paved or grassy**

This race is not for the clumsy or the shy.

Mark out start and finish lines and place them at opposite ends of the racing field, about 15 yards (13.5m) apart. Players on the same team pair off back-to-back, linking arms at the elbows and pulling bodies close together. Pairs from both teams stand sideways behind the start line, so the two inside players face each other and the two outside players face the sides of the field.

At the "Go" signal, both pairs of racers walk or run towards the finish line, all the while remaining "attached." When a pair crosses the finish line, it must revolve two-

and-a-half times before it goes back in the other direction. Now the inside "twin" becomes the outside twin and vice versa. The race back across is usually a little more wiggly after that dizzying spin!

After crossing the start line, the first pair of twins tags the second pair—waiting anxiously with linked arms—and the race continues. The first team to get all of its twins back to the start line wins the game.

Three-Legged Relay

Players:	**16–40 (8–20 on a team), but always an even number**
Materials:	**8 short lengths—24 inches (60cm)—of rope or cloth to tie racers' ankles**
	Rope or wooden stakes for marking start and finish lines
Surface:	**Grassy**

Here's a relay race guaranteed to keep both players and watchers "in stitches." You may want to practice the three-legged walk with your partner before you try it in the tournament—but part of the fun in "Three-Legged Relay" is never getting it quite right!

Mark out 15-foot (4.5m) long start and finish lines and place them at opposite ends of the racing field, about 20 yards (18m) apart. The players of each team line up in pairs, one pair behind the other, and the two teams stand seven feet (2m) apart.

Now for the fun. Each pair of players must "share a leg"—that is, the inside ankle of each player is tied to his partner's inside ankle. Use the short length of rope or cloth for this, making sure that you tie it tight enough to stay on during the race, but not so tight that it's uncomfortable.

At the "Go" signal, pairs of players from the competing teams race forward towards the finish line—each player struggling to control this "shared leg" with his racing partner. It takes a while before you get the hang of it, and a few initial moments of spinning, tripping, or just plain flopping to the ground in exasperation are to be expected!

After the players cross the finish line, they turn and race back to tag the second pair of players on their team. The second pair hobbles across and back to tag the third pair, and so on. The winner is the first team to tag its original pair of players.

Interferers

Players: 6–10
Materials: Chalk or rope for marking start and finish lines
Surface: Paved or grassy

In this game the losers get even with the winners. Draw a start and finish line 30 yards (27m) apart. Players line up behind the start line, and at the signal, sprint for the finish. The player who comes in last becomes the "Interferer" and stands in the way of the others during the next race, running into them and generally disturbing the course of the run. The player who comes in last for *this* race now joins the Interferer for the third race, and so on, until only two racers remain and all the others are Interferers.

The single racer who makes it to the other side wins the game.

Clothespin Handshake

Players: 12–24 (6–12 on a team), but always an even number

Materials: 8 clothespins
Chalk or rope for marking boundaries

Surface: Paved or grassy

Mark two starting lines 20 feet (6m) apart. Divide the teams in half, lining up half the players behind the start and half behind the finish line. Decide which side will begin and give the first in line four clothespins.

Racers tuck the clothespins between the fingers of their right hand, pressing the fingers together to secure them.

At the "Go" signal, they cross to their teammates on the opposite side, holding their right hands out in front of their bodies in a "handshake" position. At no time may a player use the left hand to help grip the clothespins.

Racers may walk or run. If a racer drops a clothespin along the way, he may pick it up but must return to the starting line and begin again. Racers who make it to the other side pass their clothespins to teammates with a "handshake"—that is, they carefully relax their fingers enough to loosen the clothespins. The receivers extend their left hands and grasp the pins between *their* fingers now—and the race continues.

The first team to switch sides completely wins the race.

Chain Gang Race

Players: 3 if single racers, 6 or 9 if racing teams
Materials: Rope, at least 30 feet (9m) long
Chalk or wooden stakes for marking start and finish lines
Surface: Paved or grassy
Special: Players must wear old pants with belt loops

Draw a start and finish line 30 yards (9m) apart. Players get together in threes. Players #1 and #2 thread the rope through a belt loop on the back of Player #2's pants. Player #2 stands at the mid-section of the rope and is able to move freely along the rope in either direction. Then Player #3 ties one end of the rope to the belt loop on the back of Player #1's pants, and Player #1 ties the other end to the back of Player #3's pants. Neither end player can move along the length of the rope.

Players line up behind the start line at enough distance from each other so that the rope is taut. At the "Go" signal, everyone races for the finish line. The fastest racer, however, is held in check by the others, and the slowest is pulled forward by the fastest. To complicate matters, the middle racer acts as a "ballast"—sliding along the length of the rope in either direction, depending on his strategy. For example: Player #2 might close the distance between himself and the fastest racer in a sprint for the finish line—an offensive move—or he might slide towards the slower player in order to "brake" the faster one—a defensive move. Of course, both end players may slow down the middle player too, so "Chain Gang Race" is an unusual combination of strategy, competition and cooperation.

Players must remain running at all times—no stopping is allowed—but they may slow down to a near-walk as long as they maintain a vigorous jogging movement.

The first player to cross the finish line wins. Players change positions on the rope for the next race.

Chariot Race

You can also turn "Chain Gang Race" into a "chariot" race between teams. In this case, three attached racers make up one team, competing with another team of three attached racers. Racers of the same team must coordinate their running efforts—a whole new challenge!

Beach Ball Relay

Racers: 13–41 (6–20 on a team), but always an even number + a referee

Materials: 2 inflatable beach balls

                Chalk or rope for marking start and finish lines

Surface: Paved, grassy or sandy—but wide

Although this game is called "Beach Ball Relay," you can substitute any lightweight ball, such as those colorful plastic ones sold in toy and sports shops.

A large area is necessary for this game—an uncrowded beach works perfectly. Draw, or mark out start and finish lines, each about 12 yards (10.8m) long. They should be placed at opposite sides of the racing field, which is 40–50 yards (36–45m) long. Teams line up behind the starting line, each racer paired off with a member of his own team. These paired teammates stand 15 feet (1.5m) from each other and toss the ball back and forth. So, at the start of this game you have the paired-off racers of the same team standing 15 feet apart, and the inside racers of opposite teams standing only six feet (1.8m) apart.

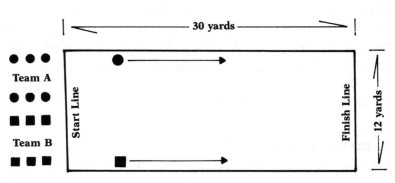

This is an interactive relay race because each team deliberately disrupts the progress of the other. At the "Go"

signal, both teams send out their first pair of racers. Each pair runs towards the finish line while tossing the ball back and forth. No more than three steps are allowed without tossing the ball or the pair goes back to the start line, so it's a good idea to have a referee. A racer from one pair may intercept a ball tossed between the other pair and throw it as far away as possible. When this happens, the racer who missed the catch chases after the ball, retrieves it, and then goes back to the starting point with his teammate to begin again. If a ball is dropped between teammates instead of intercepted, the pair returns to the starting point. Since the inside racers of opposite teams stand close to each other, deliberate bumping and tripping is not unheard of!

Each pair of racers must complete a ball toss behind the finish line before turning back. The second pair of racers waits behind the start line for the first pair to return. Then, the ball is passed (not thrown) to the second pair, and the race continues.

The first team to pass the ball back to its original pair of racers wins the game.

Pima Relay Race

Players: 13–21 (6–10 on a team) + a referee
Materials: 2 sticks for marking race points
               Chalk or rope for marking boundaries
Surface: Paved (or hard packed dirt), grassy

This race comes from the Pima Indians of the American Southwest. Originally part of an elaborate New Year's celebration, the race later developed into a test of sheer physical prowess. A less intimidating version of the game follows—perfect for runners of all levels of expertise.

Mark out two 30-yard-long (27m) parallel running courses, one for each team, and place them 10 yards (9m) apart. Between the two courses and parallel to them, draw a straight line for the referee, who takes his position there holding the two marking sticks.

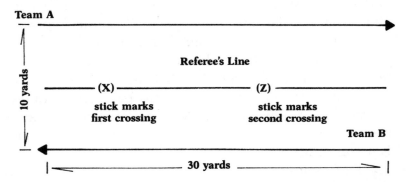

Each team splits in half and stands at opposite ends of the running courses. At a signal from the referee, the first player in line from each team runs to his teammate on the other side. Team A's first runner starts from the referee's left, Team B's first runner starts from the referee's right. Runners tag their relief on the other side and drop to the end of the line.

If the first runner from Team A outruns the first runner from Team B so that the second runner from Team A *meets B on the course*, the referee places a stick on the line at that point of meeting. If the A team maintains its lead, the third runner from Team A may *meet B's second runner on the course*, and the referee marks this second point of meeting with the other stick.

If Team A gains steadily, the two marks approach each other and finally overlap about the middle of the course. When this happens, the referee declares Team A the winner because it gained an entire lap. It's usually a tight race, though, and many runners may crisscross before one team gains the lead.

3
Cats' Eyes & Apple Pies

Marbles and marble games have been around a long time. The ancient Egyptians, who had no trouble finding hard sandy places on which to scratch gameboards, used rounded pebbles and semi-precious stones. The more practical Elizabethans knocked cherry pits; colonial Americans bowled acorns and fancy globules of painted china.

In the early Nineteenth Century, glass became

popular and glassworkers often finished a long day by "dropping marbles" for their children from the extra molten glass. But it wasn't until the turn of the century that marbles were mass produced in Akron, Ohio, and millions of them began appearing in "Five and Dime" stores across America. "Playing marbles" became a uniquely American pastime—as familiar as apple pie—and reached its peak of popularity in the 30's and 40's when a bag of milk-white "immies" (imitation agates) cost five cents and clusters of players "knuckling down" around a chalked ring were a familiar sight in almost every town.

In the early fifties, a marble factory in Pennsylvania produced a new design that soon became very popular—a clear marble with a small streak of color inside. Nicknamed "Cats' Eyes," they remain the most popular marbles for game playing.

The playing surface for a marble game is usually Spartan—hard-packed sand or dirt. But it's possible to play a dustless game on foam pads, marked permanently with the appropriate circles and lines. Foam pads make for good indoor marble playing too.

As for the games themselves, they fall into three general categories: the chase, the hole and the circle, and range from very simple to quite complicated setups. In this chapter there's a sampling of each. In all marble games, however, one general rule prevails: Any player who fails to achieve his objective—either to knock his marble into a hole or hit another player's marble—must yield to the next player.

HOW TO SHOOT A MARBLE

There are many ways to shoot a marble. Pitching it in the air or bowling it across the ground, two of the easier techniques, require little practice. But a true marble player's method of shooting, and a *must* if you're playing a game like "Ringer" is called "knuckling down." To knuckle

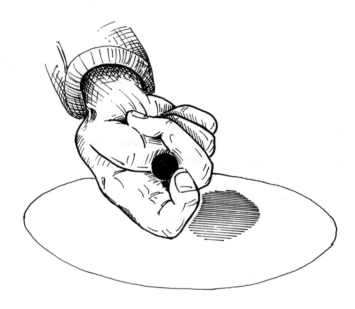

down, turn your hand palm up and place all of your knuckles (except your thumb) on the ground. Place the marble between the tip and the first joint of your first finger and hold it there by pressing against it with the nail of your thumb. When you're ready to shoot, flick your thumb outwards, propelling the marble. Watch it fly!

Bombers

Players: 2
Materials: 10 marbles for each player
Chalk or a stick for marking shoot line
Surface: Paved or hard dirt

This is an easy game for beginners and requires the "bowl" or "pitch" throw instead of the trickier "knuckle-down" technique.

Draw a shoot line behind which both players stand. The first round begins as Player #1 bowls or pitches his marble to any distance, which serves as a mark for Player #2.

Player #2 bowls his marble, trying either to hit Player #1's marble, or land within a hand's span of it. If neither occurs, both players remove their marbles and Player #1 bowls again. If Player #2 succeeds, however, he removes Player #1's marble. Now, Player #1 must throw a second time and Player #2 becomes the "Bomber." He stands over Player #1's newly tossed marble and drops, or "bombs" it with his own. If he hits the marble, he removes it. If he misses, Player #1 removes Player #2's marble.

The next round begins with sides reversed: Player #2 bowls his marble and Player #1 tries to hit it. If successful,

Player #1 removes the marble and Player #2 bowls again. Now Player #1 becomes the Bomber—a hit means he may remove the marble. A miss means he loses his marble to Player #2.

The game continues until one player runs out of marbles.

String of Beads

Players: 2
Materials: 25 marbles: 10 for each player and 5 for the beads
Chalk or a stick for drawing circle
Surface: Paved or hard dirt

In this game, "knuckling down" is the only accepted way to shoot and each player should put aside a favorite marble to use as a "shooter" for the entire game.

Draw a ring about four feet (1.2m) in diameter. Place five marbles at the center of the ring in a loop like a string of beads. Leave a little space between each "bead." The players knuckle down at the edge of the ring and shoot their marbles towards the beads. The player who comes closest without going outside the ring begins the game.

The object is to knock the beads out of the ring while keeping the shooter marble inside. A marble knocked out counts as one point for the player who shoots. He removes it and continues playing until he either misses a shot, or shoots out of the ring. When this happens, the second player takes a turn—knuckling down outside the ring to make his first shot.

The first player to collect 13 marbles wins and takes—for "keeps," or at least until the next game—all the remaining marbles in the ring.

Milkie

Players: 4

Materials: 1 marble for each player plus a white marble for the center

Chalk or a stick for drawing the square

Surface: Paved or hard dirt

This game was supposedly a favorite of Abraham Lincoln, who, legend has it, was an excellent player. It's also one of the few marble games to use a square instead of a circle. The title "Milkie" comes from the tradition of placing a white marble in the center of the square as a target for the other players, but any color marble will do—so long as it stands out easily from each player's shooter marble.

Draw a square with three-foot (.9m) sides and place the milkie in the center. Each of the four players places a shooting marble at one of the corners of the square. The first player chooses one of the remaining players to be his target and announces that player's name. Then, he knocks the milkie out of the center of the square with his shooting marble so that it ricochets into the target player's corner, bumping his marble. The target player is eliminated only if the milkie remains inside the square.

If the milkie misses its mark, or if the shooting marble misses the milkie but winds up very close to the target player's marble, the target player has a chance to get even. Now, he uses his own shooting marble to bump the first player's marble as far away as possible. If successful, he places his marble back in its original position, while the bumped first player must inch his way back into his corner during the next few turns in order to shoot again. If unsuccessful, the target player must inch back while the first player goes back to *his* original corner.

Getting even is tricky and a player shouldn't try it

unless he's close enough to knock his opponent far away. If the target player chooses not to retaliate, the first player places his marble back in its original corner and the second player takes a turn shooting at the milkie.

The challenge of the game is to calculate a shot that will bump your opponent's marble without putting your own marble in jeopardy. If you wind up within a hair's-breadth of an opponent without knocking him out of his corner, you are certain to be bumped a considerable distance by your missed target and will have to inch your way back. Though annoying, this bump will not remove you from the game. A player loses his marble and is *out* only if bumped by the milkie. He can only be eliminated when another player shoots at the milkie from his corner, making it ricochet with enough force to bump the target player's marble.

The game continues until all but one player is eliminated. The surviving player wins the game.

Ringer

Players:	**2–6**
Materials:	**13 marbles and 2–6 shooter marbles, depending on the number of players**
	Chalk or a stick for drawing the circle
Surface:	**Paved or hard dirt**

This is the most widely played marble game and provides a good opportunity to bone up on shooting technique.

Draw a ring on the ground, ten feet (3m) in diameter. With the center of the ring as a point of intersection, draw two lines, each two feet (.6m) long, at right angles to form a cross. Place a marble at the center and three marbles on each of the four lines of the cross, each marble no less than three inches from the next one.

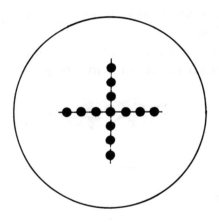

To win, a player must knock seven marbles out of the ring while keeping his shooting marble inside the ring. He takes the first shot from any point outside the ring and continues shooting until he either wins, misses or shoots out of the ring. If he doesn't win on the first try—and he usually doesn't—the next player takes a turn.

For each new turn, a player takes his first shot from any point outside the ring. And of course, all shots are performed "knuckles down" to count!

Losing Your Marbles

Players:	2–4
Materials:	10 marbles for each player + one target marble
	Stick for marking shoot line
	Garden spade or old spoon for digging
Surface:	Hard packed sand

Dig a small hole about six inches (15cm) in diameter and two inches (5cm) deep. One marble, belonging to neither player, is placed in the hole as a target. Draw a shoot line 15 feet (4.5m) from the hole. From here, players take turns tossing their marbles with the object of hitting—or "banging"—the target marble in the hole three times.

The first player to reach that magic number picks up and gets to keep all the marbles that missed. The game continues as players gradually "lose their marbles" to the winner.

Potty

Players:	2–5
Materials:	20 marbles for each player
	Stick for marking shoot line
	Garden spade or old spoon for digging
Surface:	Hard packed sand

Winning a game of "Potty" requires both aggressiveness and restraint. It's a game where the tables may turn easily and no one is quite sure who'll turn out to be the champion.

Make the hole, or "potty" six inches (15cm) in diameter and two inches (5cm) deep. Place the shoot line not less than seven but not more than ten feet (2m–3m) away. To begin the game, each player throws his marble at the potty from behind the shoot line. The marble that comes closest without falling in wins for its thrower the privilege of "opening shot."

The object of the game is to get into the potty, if you can—but not *close* to it. Players take turns throwing their marbles until one lucky player gets into the potty. That player collects all marbles that fall within a hand's span from the potty's edge. The marbles that lie at a distance greater than a hand's span return to their owners. Then it's the next player's turn.

If an opening shot goes into the potty, the other players must each surrender one marble to the opening shooter before the next player is up.

There's a twist in this game. Although a player might want his marble in the potty so that he can collect other marbles close by, once he's in, he's at the mercy of the next player who has three chances to knock him and take his marble.

The game continues as player after player runs out of marbles and drops out. Eventually, winner takes all.

Poison

Players: 2–5
Materials: 20 marbles per player
Stick for drawing the circle
Garden spade or old spoon for digging
Surface: Hard packed sand

Poison gives a good player the chance to become truly deadly.

Dig a shallow hole with a diameter of about five inches (12.5cm). This is the "Poison Pot" and each player drops a marble into it. Next, draw a circle around the hole with a radius of three feet (.9m) from the hole's edge. This is called the "Poison Ring." The setup is complete when players place additional marbles within the ring—2 each—in a circular formation around the poison pot.

Players knuckle down five feet (1.5m) from the ring and shoot to see who comes closest to the ring's edge without going over the line. The most accurate shot entitles the shooter to take a place just outside the ring and begin the game.

POISON—PART 1

The rules of Poison dictate that a player must shoot a marble out of the ring, and his shooter marble must also leave the ring. Marbles that leave the ring become his property and count as one point each. If he fails—by missing a target, or if his shooting marble remains inside—he surrenders to the poison pot all of the marbles he won on that turn, and the turn is over. If he fails on the first attempt and has no winning marbles to surrender, he must pay a penalty of two marbles to the Poison Pot.

When a sharp-shooting player collects ten marbles and scores ten points, he calls out "Poison!" and the game pauses. He distributes his ten marbles among the other players, who remove the rest of their marbles from the ring and wait for the next part of the game.

POISON—PART 2

The Poison Player now removes all the marbles in the Poison Pot and places them around the outside of the ring. Then each remaining player, one by one, is called to place all of his marbles inside the ring as targets for the Poison Player.

The Poison Player shoots, without interruption, his poison marbles from outside the ring, bumping and eliminating the other player's marbles. If the Poison Player misses, the player who is his target gets to remove his remaining marbles from the ring and the *next* player is called to throw in *his* marbles.

It might seem like an excruciating way to wind down a game—the remaining players having little hope of saving their marbles from the Poison Player—if it weren't for one trick rule. If the Poison Player accidentally shoots a marble into the Poison Pot, he is no longer poison and his victim becomes the new Poison Player—taking whatever marbles remain in the center and arranging them, just as the first Poison Player did—outside the ring. Now this *new* Poison Player calls for the remaining players to toss all their marbles into the ring.

The game continues until one Poison Player—the winner—collects all the marbles.

4
Take the Ball & *Run!*

If you enjoy running, playing ball, tagging and being tagged as separate activities—you'll love the games in this chapter because they combine the *best parts* of all your favorites. One game, from Colonial times, even throws in a bit of Hide-and-Seek!

You'll find games here for soccerballs, softballs, baseballs—games to play on grass or pavement; familiar and unfamiliar games requiring a wide range of tossing skills and strategy-making; and games for mixed age groups.

Great games all!

Greek Ball Game _____

Players: **10–20 (5–10 on a team)**
Materials: **Medium-sized inflated ball (or soccerball, basketball, etc.)**
             Chalk or rope for marking boundaries
Surface: **Paved or grassy**

Here's a game that's as interesting to watch as it is to play. Find a wide flat area with no bumps or holes and mark out the playing field—a 20-foot (6m) square. Divide the square into four quadrants and at the center intersection place the ball. Separate players into two equal teams and line them up just behind the boundary lines on opposite sides of the square. Place the ball in the center of the court.

    The first player on team A's line prepares to run and the last player on team B's line prepares to run, so that the runners of each team stand in opposite corners of the square.

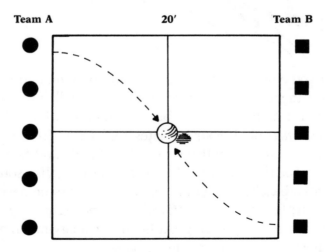

    At the signal, the two runners dash to the center of the square to gain possession of the ball. If Team A's runner gets there first, he picks up the ball and attempts to throw it over the heads of Team B and over the boundary line. Team B may not step into the square but must catch or deflect the ball from behind the line.

If the runner's first throw gets through, Team A gets a point. If it doesn't, Team B keeps the ball in play by tossing it back to its own runner, who remains in the center. Now Team B's runner attempts to throw the ball over the heads of Team A to score a point.

After the first point, set up the game again. The original runners go to the end of the line, and the next players in line become the two new runners.

The team with the highest score after a half-hour of playing wins the game.

Corner Ball

Players:	**12–20 (6–10 on a team)**
Materials:	**Medium-sized inflated ball (or soccerball, basketball, etc.)**
	Chalk, rope or stick for marking boundaries
Surface:	**Paved, grassy or sandy**

Goalies occupy all four corners of the 25 × 40 foot (7.5m × 12m) playing field—a challenging situation for both scoring and strategy.

Divide the field in half with a center line and mark off a four-by-four-foot (1.2m × 1.2m) square in each of the corners. All but two players from each team line up five feet (1.5m) from, and at opposite sides of the center line. The two remaining players of each team become the goalies who stand in the corner squares of the opposing team. Goalies may step outside their squares provided they keep one foot or hand inside at all times.

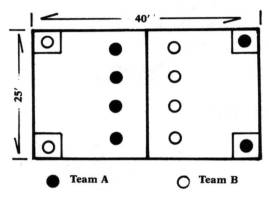

Team A   Team B

Teams toss a coin for the opening serve. The ball is thrown—by anyone on the serving team—over the center line to the receiving team. Once the ball is in motion, players score one point each time they manage to throw it over the heads of the opposing team to one of the goalies. The goalie throws the ball back to his team and the playing continues until one team reaches a score of 21.

Teammates may pass the ball to one another or may intercept a goalie's throw, but no player may step inside the goalie's square or over the center line. If this happens, the offending team loses one point and the serve goes to the other team.

Highball

Players: 10–20
Materials: Medium-sized inflated ball (or soccerball, basketball, etc.)
Chalk or rope
Surface: Paved or grassy

Of Native American ancestry, "Highball"—a kind of free-for-all, "no frills" football—will warm you up on a chilly winter afternoon.

Mark off a field, 60 × 20 feet (18m × 6m), and divide it with a center line. Players stand in a group at the center of the field. One player tosses the ball high in the air and tries to catch it along with the other players. Whoever catches the ball runs to either end line and scores a point if he crosses it. Other players try to intercept the ball by tackling the running player and running for the point. A running player, if threatened, may pass the ball to another player and then join in chasing him—the chased suddenly becoming the chaser!

Whenever a player scores a point, all players regroup in the center and the scoring player is the one to toss the ball in the air. The player with the highest score after an agreed-upon time period wins the game.

Haley-Over (Wall Ball)

Players:	**9–17 (4 to 8 on a team) + a referee**
Materials:	**Softball**
Surface:	**Paved or grassy**
Special:	**A wall or small building is necessary, high enough to hide the teams from each other**

One of the most exciting sports to come down to us from colonial America, "Haley-Over," sometimes called "Wall Ball," is a kind of blind-man's-bluff tagging game—full of suspense and surprises!

Teams stand on opposite sides of the wall or small building, completely hidden from each other. A player throws the ball over the top to any height and in any direction. If the players on the other side miss the catch, they return the ball over the wall and the volley continues until someone from either team makes a catch.

The player who catches the ball then races around the corner to tag players of the other team who scatter in all directions. The chaser has 30 seconds to tag a runner by throwing the ball and hitting him, or by chasing and touching him with the ball. The referee calls "Time!" at that point and if no one is tagged, the chaser returns to his side.

A tagged runner joins the chasing team on the other side of the wall. Now the chasing team throws the ball over and the routine is repeated.

"Haley-Over" calls on the honor system, since the throwing team has no way of knowing whether or not the opposing team caught the ball on the fly. Only then may a player come around to the other side to tag the throwing team.

When all players wind up on one side, the game ends.

Piggyback Ball _____

Players: 10–20 (5–10 on a team)
Materials: Medium-sized inflated ball (or soccerball, basketball, etc.)
Surface: Grassy

Players divide into two teams: the Horses and the Riders. The Horses carry the Riders piggyback. The game starts when one Rider tosses the ball to any other Rider who must catch it without fumbling. Of course, the Horses make it difficult for Riders to throw the ball accurately by running and spinning around!

When a Rider drops the ball, all Riders jump from

their Horses and scatter. The nearest Horse picks up the ball and throws it to any other Horse or at one of the running Riders. If this Horse hits the Rider with a single throw, he scores one point for the Horses—who now become the Riders. If the throw misses, the Riders jump back on their Horses and the game continues as before.

The first team to score a total of 10 points wins.

Pass the Ball

Players: 10–20 (5–10 on a team)
Materials: Medium-sized inflated ball
Surface: Paved or grassy

Players divide into two teams and stand facing each other in two equal rows. Position the rows at least five feet (1.5m) from each other—closer together for younger players and farther apart for "experts."

The first thrower, at the head of either line, tosses the ball to the player standing directly opposite him. That thrower tosses the ball to the player in the opposite row, second in line from the original thrower. The resulting ball toss pattern looks like this:

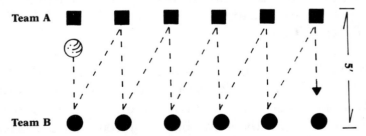

When the last player catches the ball, he returns it to the player opposite him and the tossing continues in the opposite direction.

When a player misses a catch, he takes one step backwards and continues playing from this position. A second missed catch is another step backwards, and a third missed catch eliminates him from the game. When a player has stepped back but manages to catch and return the ball without dropping it, he may take one step forward each time until back in line.

The team that has the largest number of players remaining after 10 minutes wins the game.

Circle Ball Race

Players: 10–20 (5–10 on a team)
Materials: Two medium-sized inflated balls
Surface: Paved, grassy or sandy

Simple rules make this game fun for even the youngest players, though everyone appreciates the fast-paced excitement of "Circle Ball Race."

Each team stands in a circle and appoints a captain. The distance between players in the circle should depend on the throwing skills of the players—more distance for skilled throwers and less for beginners.

One team's captain shouts "Go" and the game begins as captains of both teams toss the ball to the players on the right, who toss it to players on *their* right, and so on, around the circle. Captains call out "One!" to signify that the ball has made one complete revolution and continue counting out each round as it is completed. You can vary the game by tossing the ball for the first revolution, rolling it for the second, bouncing it for the third, kicking it for the fourth—as fancy a routine as you'd like.

The first captain to count five revolutions holds the ball high over his head—his team wins the race.

Bangball

Players: 9–17 (4–8 on a team) + a referee to call out
numbers

Materials: Medium-sized inflated ball (or soccerball,
basketball, etc.)

Chalk, rope or stick for marking boundaries

Surface: Paved, grassy or sandy

Mark out a 20 × 20 foot (6m × 6m) square for a playing
field and place the ball at the center. The players, except for
the referee, divide into two equal teams. Each team counts

off consecutively so that every player has a number. The teams line up in numerical order on opposite sides of the square, just in back of the boundary lines.

The game begins when the referee calls out a number. The two players from the opposing teams who share that number race for the ball in the center. When one of the players reaches the ball, both players freeze.

The player with the ball now has one chance to throw, or "bang" the other player for a game point. If he succeeds, or if the other player moves from his spot while dodging the ball, the thrower's team gets a point. If the other player catches the ball, a point goes to his team. If the ball misses the target player, neither team scores.

After the first throw, which may or may not result in a game point, players return to their lines and wait for the referee to call out a new number.

The first team to score 21 points wins the game.

Circle Dodge Ball

Players: 10–20 (5–10 on a team)
Materials: Medium-sized inflated ball
Surface: Paved, grassy or sandy

This game might seem ruthless in its final stages, but it guarantees a rollicking good time for everyone.

Players break into two teams. Team A has the ball and forms a loose circle around Team B. At the signal, players of Team A begin throwing the ball at the players of Team B, who dodge it to avoid being hit.

Team B's players may not catch the ball, but may roll it back out if it stops within the circle. When more than one player is hit, only the first is out—"out" means leaving the center and joining the throwers of Team A.

You guessed it. Soon the throwers clearly outnumber the dodgers, and you have to be pretty quick on your feet to be last one out—the winner.

For the next game, Team B circles Team A.

"Spauldeen" Tennis

Players: 8–16 (4–8 on a team)
Materials: 1 "Spauldeen," or standard tennis ball
Chalk for marking boundaries
Surface: Paved

For any serious street or schoolyard ball player, the name "Spauldeen" should ring a bell. Manufactured by the Spaulding Company, the size, weight and bounce of this pink rubber ball make it perfect for just about anything. If you can't find one in your local sporting goods or novelty shop, a tennis ball will do almost as well.

Draw a court, 50 × 20 feet (15m × 6m) and divide it in half. Teams take opposite sides of the court and flip a coin to determine which team serves first. Players of each team spread out over the court, and whoever serves may do so from wherever he or she stands.

The game begins when the first server bounces the ball once, and then slaps it with his palm over the center line to the other team's court. The other team's players attempt to return the ball by hitting it back the same way. If they miss, drop, or slap the ball out-of-bounds, the servers score a point. If they return the ball successfully, the volley continues until one team fumbles the ball, scoring for the other team.

Whichever team gets a point serves for the next round. The first team to gain 21 points wins the game.

Punchball

Players: 8–20
Materials: Medium-sized inflated ball
Surface: Paved, grassy or sandy

Good for the reflexes, the passing and faking techniques of "Punchball" may remind you of, and are good training for, a more familiar game—football.

The players form a circle with three or four feet (about 1m) between players. One player, "It," remains outside the circle. A circle player begins the game by quickly passing the ball—either by handing it or tossing it—to the player on his right or left. Players continue to pass the ball around in any direction, but it may not be tossed across the circle or skip a player as it goes around.

"It" chases the ball as it moves around, trying to punch it into the center of the circle as it moves between players. Players may fake movements left or right to keep "It" on his toes. If the ball falls to the ground, the last player to touch it may pick it up and start passing it again.

When "It" succeeds in punching the ball into the center, the last player who passed it becomes the new "It."

Play usually continues until everyone has a chance to be "It."

Spud

Players: 4–10
Materials: Medium-sized inflated ball
Surface: Paved

Players may either take numbers or use their own names. All form a circle around one player who has the ball. That player throws the ball straight up into the air and calls the number or name of another player. Everyone scatters except for the named player, who catches the ball and calls out "Spud!"—freezing all the others.

The named player now takes three giant steps to the closest frozen player and attempts to tag him by throwing or rolling the ball. If successful, the tagged player gets an "S" and throws the ball in the next round.

If the thrower misses her target, she gets an "S" and tries again. The second, third, and fourth time players either get tagged or miss tagging someone, they get the letters "P," "U," and "D" respectively. Any player to spell "SPUD" is out of the game.

Continue playing until all but two players remain. The first to get the other out wins the game.

5

Baseball, Basketball & Family

Baseball has a huge family, and quite a few distinguished ancestors. "Rounders," the great-granddaddy of modern baseball, began in England where players still keep it alive. Offspring of the baseball family live in Russia, Africa and China now, and there's just no telling how far they'll roam.

One thing's for sure—you won't find a more flexible game! You can mix age groups and genders, organize a game between teams or individual players, and do just about anything, anywhere.

Basketball, too, has all the ingredients for a rousing good time. These games are also great warmups for the big leagues.

Peggyball

Players: 2

Materials: "Peggyball," or a golfball-sized wooden ball you can purchase in lumberyards

Broomstick or pool cue, sawed off to 2 feet (.6m)

12 inches × 2 inches (30cm × 5cm) wooden riser, shaved to a point at one end

2 inches (5cm) strip of wood for lip

Short dowel or stick, 1 inch (2.5cm) in diameter

Surface: Paved or hard packed dirt

A homespun relative of baseball, "Peggyball," also known as "Cat" or "Trapball," first appeared in Fall River, Massachusetts, around 1865.

Making a Peggyball & Other Equipment

Look for your peggyball in lumberyards that carry ornamental wood pieces—wooden balls, with a hole drilled in one side, that are often used for decorating the ends of dowels, banisters and curtain rods. Plug up the drilled hole with wood putty and allow your peggyball to dry for several days.

Next, find a piece of wood for the riser and shave one end to a point. At the blunt edge, glue the wooden lip and allow to dry. Place the riser on the dowel "seesaw-style" so that the pointed end is off the ground and the peggyball rests on the blunt end.

To hit a peggyball, strike the pointed end of the riser with your broomstick, flipping it into the air.

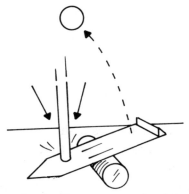

Then wallop the ball out into the blue yonder with your broomstick. You can't imagine the sound!

Players take turns batting. The batter estimates how far the ball travelled and calls out a number in increments of five. For example, if the ball comes to rest 15 feet from the batter, three points are at stake. The opponent must decide whether he can retrieve the ball in the three steps (or leaps) and collect the three points—or pass, in which case the batter receives the points.

If a player strikes out by missing the peggyball three times in a row, he changes places with his opponent, who automatically gets one point.

The first player to score 21 points wins the game.

Horse _____

Players: **2–5**
Materials: **Basketball**
Surface: **Basketball court**

This enjoyable game developed from one of those "bone-up-on-your-shot" exercises—it's great for warming up, too.

The first player takes a shot from anywhere on the court. If he or she gets it into the basket, the other players must duplicate the same shot from the same location. If they all succeed, the first player makes a second, and usually more challenging shot. If one of the other players fails to duplicate the first player's shot, that player gets the letter "H."

If the first player misses a shot, the second player has the opportunity to make a shot that must be imitated by the other players.

The game continues as players accumulate letters for missed shots. Players who spell out HORSE are out of the game. The remaining player wins.

Tee Ball

Players:	**18 (9 to a team)**
Materials:	**Softball**
	Bat
	Cardboard tube, 3 feet (.9m) long or a commercially bought "Tee"
	Trash can covers or cardboard for marking bases
Surface:	**Sandy or grassy**

"Tee Ball" is a great introduction to baseball because it teaches young players the rules of the game and helps them develop skills for playing it. No team wins or loses, which allows beginning players to enjoy learning the basics—batting, throwing, catching and fielding—without the pressure of competing.

Little League stores sell the rubber "tee," but for an inexpensive substitute, you can remove the cardboard tube from a roll of gift-wrap and place the end in a soft mound of sand where the batter swings. The tee should stand about three feet (.9m) high, tip over easily when the batter hits the ball from the top, and substitute for pitched throws.

Scale the playing field to fit younger players: 60 feet (18m) between bases and 46 feet (13.8m) between home plate and the pitcher's mound. Teams take turns batting or fielding, the fielders having the usual nine positions as follows:

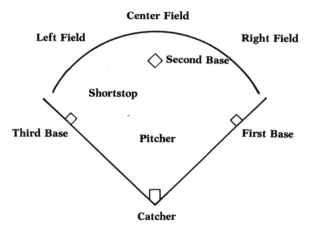

Each player may keep his field position for the entire game or players can trade positions for variety.

As in baseball, teams score points when the batter hits the ball and runs through the bases. A player may run only when he or a teammate hits the ball. Runners who make it through all three bases and back to home plate score a point for their team. Unlike baseball, however, points measure a team's progress in learning basic batting skills *only*—nothing is tallied—no team wins or loses.

The fielding team attempts to tag out a batter by either catching the ball "on the fly" (before it hits the

Baseball, Basketball & Family • *71*

ground), or catching it after it rolls or bounces and throwing it to the player on the base the runner is approaching. For instance, if the third baseman catches the ball and tags the runner before he reaches third base, the runner is out and the batting team scores no point. If the runner touches third base before the baseman can catch the ball and tag him, he continues to home plate and scores a point for his team. Fielders may tag out runners on any base—including home plate, by throwing the ball to the catcher—in this way.

In regulation baseball, three "strikes"—or three balls missed by the batter—count as an "out." In "Tee Ball," however, every player up to bat swings as many times as he or she likes until connecting with the ball. The next in line then takes a turn. When everyone on the batting team makes a successful hit, the teams switch sides.

When a team bats once and plays the field once, this makes up an inning. Play four innings—six at most. The usual nine innings tend to exhaust younger players.

Lapkta (Russian Baseball) ———

Players: **12–20 (6–10 on a team)**
Materials: **Softball**
                Bat
                Chalk, rope or stick for marking boundary lines
Surface: **Paved, grassy, or hard-packed dirt.**

Maybe it's a little unfair to compare "Lapkta" with American-style baseball—it was played by czars and peasants alike, long before Babe Ruth ever stepped up to bat!

Mark out a rectangular playing field 20 × 50 yards

(18m × 45m), creating two end zone boundaries, opposite each other, at the narrow sides of the field. The first team up to bat lines up against one of these boundaries, while the other team spreads out on the field in the formation shown below—the "pitcher" standing five yards (4.5m) from the batting team.

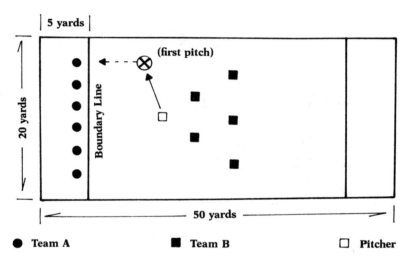

Each team counts off to establish batting order. Then the pitcher pitches the ball to the first batter. If the first batter misses, he passes the bat to the player on his right. If the next player misses, he passes the bat to *his* right, and so on, until everyone in line has a turn. If no one hits the ball, the batters get a zero score and change places with the fielders for the next "inning."

When a batter hits the ball, everyone on his team sprints across the field to safety behind the end zone on the other side. The fielding team scrambles to catch the ball and then to tag players of the other team—either by throwing the ball or touching the runners with it. Fielders may also throw the ball to other fielders in order to tag runners out of direct reach. Tagged players stand to the side and wait to be counted before the next inning begins.

Each tagged player counts as one point for the fielding team.

The next inning begins with the fielders up to bat and the batters in the field.

All in all, this is a fast-moving, terrific game. The team with the highest score after nine innings wins.

Half-Ball Baseball

Players:	6–18 (3–9 on a team)
Materials:	Broom handle bat
	Spauldeen ball (or another kind of hollow rubber ball), cut in half
Surface:	Paved

Cutting an old ball in half might seem a little strange, but is gives a fun and challenging twist to an old favorite.

You can make your own half-ball by cutting a Spauldeen ball in half. Find a fine-toothed hacksaw and some-one to saw it in half for you, if you're not familiar with the tool yourself. Some sports stores carry commercial half-balls, if you don't want to fuss with making your own.

Take an old broom handle and wrap one end in masking or electrical tape so you can get a good grip on it.

After you form two teams and count out to establish batting order, the batters stand in line while the fielders stand wherever they please, 40 feet (12m) away. The first batter tosses the half-ball in the air and swings. If he connects, the ball skims through the air like a wobbling Frisbee in anything but a straight line!

Fielders scramble to catch the ball on the fly and put the batter "out," but one bounce on the street counts as a single for the batting team; two bounces, a double; three bounces, a triple; and four bounces a home-run. If a flying half-ball is strange to see, a bouncing half-ball is stranger. Fielders collide with one another trying to grab it!

When a batter misses his own toss, he "strikes." Three strikes and the teams switch sides. The team with the higher score after an agreed-upon amount of time wins the game.

Kickball

Players:	**12–18 (6–9 on a team)**
Materials:	**Medium-sized inflated ball**
	Mats, cardboard or trash can lids for bases, or chalk to draw them
Surface:	**Paved or grassy**

"Kickball," a kind of no-props baseball, doesn't require highly developed hitting or running skills.

The playing field consists of a baseball diamond with 25 feet (7.5m) between each of the three bases, adjustable for younger players. One team bats while the other team fields and pitches. The players in the field take the usual positions: one player to each of the three bases, plus at least one infield and one outfield player.

The pitcher rolls the ball to the kicker, who stands at home plate. The kicker rarely "strikes out" on a rolled ball, so two foul balls kicked in succession count as one strike. As in baseball, three strikes (six foul balls) make an "out." After three outs, or half an inning—teams switch sides.

When a player kicks the ball, he or she runs for first base while the fielders scramble to catch the ball and put the runner out in one of four ways:

- Catching a fly ball
- Throwing a ball to the player on first base, who will touch the base before the runner reaches it
- Tagging the runner with the ball
- Hitting the runner by throwing the ball

Since an inflated rubber ball will not travel very far when kicked high in the air, and the opposing team can easily catch it, it's best to kick hard and low to the ground—aim to shoot between fielders.

If a runner makes it home after touching all three bases, he or she scores a point for the team.

The team with the most points at the end of nine innings wins the game.

Around the World

Players: **2–5**
Materials: **Basketball**
             Tape to mark positions
Surface: **Basketball court**

Tape seven evenly spaced "X's" to the floor in a semicircular pattern around the basketball hoop, none closer than 20 feet. Player #1 shoots from the first X. If the ball goes through, he moves to the second X, and so on, until he misses, at which point he loses his turn and Player #2 begins on the first X.

When Player #1's turn comes up again, he continues

shooting from the X where he left off and continues "around the world" until he misses a shot. Player #2 then shoots from where he left off, and the game proceeds until one player has moved across all seven X's and back again.

Greedy

Players: **3 (2 + a referee)**
Materials: **2 basketballs**
                 Chalk or tape
Surface: **Basketball court**

Mark an "X" on one of the basketballs with chalk or tape. Each player uses his own ball and may never touch the ball of his opponent.

The two players begin shooting baskets at the same time from anywhere on the court. The referee keeps score. The first "greedy" player to get 10 baskets wins.

If in the heat of play, a player accidentally picks up his opponent's ball and shoots with it, he automatically loses. The game moves so quickly, though, that no one remains a loser for long!

6
Rolling Bowling Games

Sometimes a ball on the ground is worth two in the air. We guarantee you'll have so much fun playing these "Rolling Bowling Games" that you just might retire your pitching arm!

Garontki

Players: 3–6 (2–5 + a referee)
Materials: Broom handle, sawed off to 3 feet (.9m) (throwing-baton)
5 medium-sized wooden building blocks
Chalk or stick for marking boundaries
Surface: Paved or hard-packed dirt

This unusual game from Russia uses wooden blocks for bowling pins and a throwing baton instead of a ball.

Draw a boundary line, 10 feet (3m) long, for the players to stand behind. Then, draw a four-foot (1.2m) square 40 feet (12m) away where the referee will set up the blocks.

There are five block designs, each at another level of difficulty.

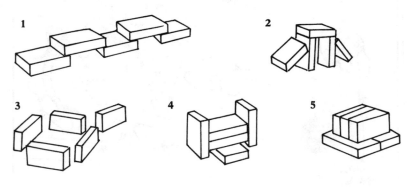

After the referee assembles the first design, he calls for the first player. Each player throws his baton—not as a spear, but with a spinning motion by holding the end. He has two chances to knock all of the blocks completely out of the square for a total of five points. If he knocks all the blocks out on the first throw, that player also gets a five-point bonus for a total of 10 points. Then the referee calls for the next player.

After each player has thrown and accumulated points in the first round, the referee sets up the blocks in design #2. Again, players take turns throwing the baton at the blocks and tallying points.

For the third round the referee sets up design #3, and so on, until the players have knocked down all five designs.

The player with the highest score at the end of five rounds wins the game.

Bounce-Off Bowling _____

Players:	2–6
Materials:	**Medium-sized inflated ball (or soccerball, basketball, etc.)**
	10 large plastic soda bottles
	Chalk or rope for marking starting line
Surface:	**Flat paved or grassy, with nearby wall**

You can either bowl or toss the ball in this "knock 'em down" game. Try to find a flat surface and sturdy wall for the ricochet shots.

At a distance of 10 feet (3m) in front of the wall, arrange the soda bottles in a circle eight feet (2.4m) in diameter. Make sure you separate the bottles just enough for the ball to pass through the circle. Mark a starting line for the players, 10 feet (3m) long and 20 feet (6m) from the edge of the circle.

Players, in turn, stand behind the starting line. A player may stand either at the middle of the starting line or at one of the ends, depending upon the direction in which he chooses to bowl his ball. For instance, a ball may either pass through the circle before hitting the wall, or roll beside the circle before hitting the wall, but only the bottles knocked down *after* the ball ricochets off the wall count for points. Bottles knocked over before the ball hits the wall count against you.

Each player takes three turns, knocking over as many bottles as possible for points. After three turns, total the score and set the bottles up again. The next player begins a new round.

For a more forceful and vigorous bowling game, you can weigh down the plastic bottles by pouring a little sand or water in each one.

The first player to reach a score of 21 wins the game.

Save the Fortress

Players:	**11–21 (5–10 on a team) + a referee to call innings**
Materials:	**Medium-sized inflated ball (or soccerball, basketball, etc.)**
	Large plastic soda bottles, one for each player
	Chalk, rope or stick for marking boundaries
Surface:	**Paved, grassy or sandy**

In this game, each team scrambles to "save the fortress"—actually, a wall of soda bottles.

Mark out a field 40 × 15 feet (12m × 4.5m) and divide it down the middle with a line. Create two end zones, three feet (1m) wide, at each side of the field. Divide the soda bottles in half and line them up, evenly spaced about two feet (.6m) apart, in each end zone. Each team occupies one half of the field. Teams line up on opposite sides of the center line as the game begins. A player may not enter the end zones at any time during the game.

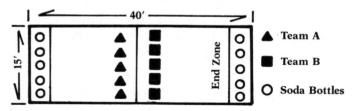

A player from Team A serves the ball across the center line into Team B's territory, trying to knock down as many bottles as possible. They do this by aiming the ball over their opponents' heads, through their legs, or between their bodies. You can imagine what the other team must do to keep that from happening!

After an agreed upon number of minutes—say three—the referee will call the end of the round and the playing stops. At this point he tabulates the score by counting the number of bottles knocked down on each side. The next round begins with a player from Team B serving over the center line into Team A territory. Again, after an agreed upon number of minutes, the referee calls "time" and adds up the points.

The team with the most points after nine rounds of play wins the game.

Half-Ball Bowling (Bowls) _____

Players: 2–5
Materials: **Solid foam ball, cut in half**
                15 empty soda cans
Surface: **Paved or hard-packed dirt**

"Half-Ball Bowling" or "Bowls" comes from the days of bowling on the green when King George III of England outlawed indoor gaming parlors. In an unusual twist from the straightforward bowling game, Half-Ball Bowling uses—what else?—half a ball!

You can find a soccer-sized solid foam ball in toy rather than sports shops. To cut the ball in half, use a fine-tooth hacksaw and find someone who knows how to use it safely, if you're not familiar with the tool yourself. Cut the ball evenly in half, so that your half ball will be smooth, balanced, and spin on its side with enough momentum to knock over the empty soda cans.

Arrange the soda cans in a wide circle, evenly spaced, about 20 feet (6m) from where the first bowler stands.

To bowl a half-ball, balance it in the palm of either hand with the flat side facing out. Bowl by rolling the ball off the palm either slightly to the left or slightly to the right (depending on which hand you use) of the soda can circle.

Bowlers take turns. The half-ball skitters around the pins and topples them from the opposite side. How does this happen? It loses momentum and leans to its round side, curving like a boomerang!

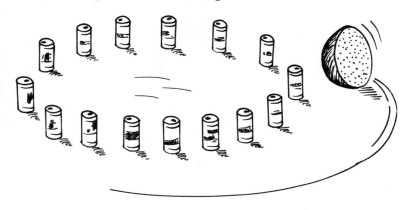

Players have two chances to roll the half-ball. They get one point for each can knocked over. If bowlers topple a can head-on, they forfeit their turn and lose whatever points were scored during it.

Player #2 stands by the cans and "spots" for Player #1—keeping score and setting up the cans after the second roll. Then it's Player #2's turn.

If more than two players bowl, Player #3 spots for Player #2; Player #4 spots for Player #3; and so on, until Player #1 spots for the last player.

The first player to get 50 points wins the game.

Flamingos

Players:	8–20 (4–10 on a team)
Materials:	3 medium-sized inflated balls (or soccerballs, basketballs, etc.)
	Chalk or rope for marking starting line
Surface:	Paved or grassy

Divide the players into two teams, Flamingos and Hunters. Draw a boundary line behind which the Hunters stand, 20 feet from the Flamingos. Both sides line up facing each other.

Hunters accumulate points by bowling at the Flamingos, who stand on one foot and may not lean against anything for support. Each Hunter bowls three times. Flamingos may hop around to avoid the ball, but if a Flamingo is hit, or touches two feet to the ground, the Hunters gain a point.

After three bowls or one "set," the Hunters and Flamingos switch sides. The team with the highest score after 10 sets wins the game.

Bottle Ball

Players:	10–20
Materials:	**Medium-sized inflated ball (or soccerball, basketball, etc.)**
	Large plastic soda bottles, one less than the number of players
	Chalk or stick for scratching boundaries
Surface:	**Paved or sandy**

Place the soda bottles in any arrangement, no bottle closer than 15 feet (4.5m) to another. Draw a circle four feet (1.2m) in diameter around each bottle. Each player, except for the one chosen to be "It," stands with one foot inside the circle, guarding his or her bottle. "It" stands anywhere—but at least six feet (1.8m) away from the nearest player.

"It" kicks the ball into one of the circles in an attempt to knock down a bottle. The remaining players protect their bottles by deflecting kicks, but must keep one foot inside the circle at all times. When "It" tumbles a bottle, he changes places with the player in whose circle it stood.

Continue until all players have a chance to be "It."

Roll-Ball

Players:	5–10
Materials:	Laundry baskets, one for each player
	A lightweight medium-sized inflated ball
	Marbles or stones for keeping score
Surface:	Paved, grassy or sandy
Special:	If playing on a sandy surface, dig holes in the sand to substitute for laundry baskets.

An interesting combination of basketball, bowling, and golf, "Roll Ball" comes from colonial New England, where it was played on country greens in the summer and in snowy fields in the winter.

Players count off and line up beside one another, each player standing in back of his basket or hole. Player #1 takes the ball, stands in front of the others at a distance of 15 feet (4.5m), and has three chances to roll or throw the ball so that it winds up in one of the baskets or holes. When he baskets a ball, everyone scatters except for the player who owns the basket. That player snatches the ball and chases the others, attempting to tag a runner by hitting him or her with the ball. If the chaser is successful, he places a marble in the tagged runner's basket. If unsuccessful, he places a marble in his own basket.

If Player #1 misses a basket on his third try, he places a marble in his own basket and tries to live down the humiliation. Player #2 rolls next, repeating the same routine.

A player is out when he accumulates five marbles in his basket. The last remaining player wins the game.

7
Novelty Games

Novelty game items were once a staple in every well-equipped candy store. What "Mom and Pop" outfit would dare run low on a supply of jacks, marbles, or wooden tops? But times have changed—sort of. Though it might be a little more difficult to find tops these days, Hula-hoops are still alive and plentiful. The same goes for Frisbees, rubber balls, jump ropes, chalk—all kinds of game-inspiring goodies!

Still, we've broadened the term "novelty" to include games that are just plain novel—strange as well as fun, different as well as familiar. Some require a little preparation, but you won't be disappointed.

Streamer Ball

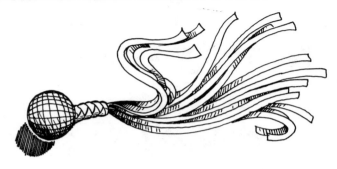

If you think there's nothing new under the sun when it comes to ball playing—think again. Just tossing a streamer ball between two players is a lot of fun—not to mention all the new games.

You can toss a streamer ball anywhere—in the street, at the park or on the beach. It's easy and inexpensive to make one—and half the fun!

Constructing a Streamer Ball

Materials: **Solid rubber softball**
Orange sack—the netted kind
Old sheet
Dye (optional)

Cut a one-and-a-half foot (45cm) square of netting from the orange sack.

Then cut the old sheet into 11 strips—each strip anywhere from three to six feet (1.2m–1.8m) long and one inch (25mm) wide. Cut a shorter strip one foot (30cm) long. If you're using a white or very pale sheet, you may want to dye the long strips vivid colors and allow them to dry before continuing.

Lay the square of orange sack on a flat surface and place the rubber ball in the center.

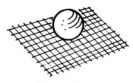

Fold the corners around the ball so that it's completely enclosed and twist the extra netting tightly to make a snug fit.

At the point where the twist is close against the ball, tie the shorter strip of sheet, knotting it several times. The ball should be tightly encased by the net now, and there should be five inches (12.5cm) of extra twisted net sticking out from the knot. Untwist the extra net and stretch it open so that it looks like a "dress." Trim the strip to about one inch (2.50cm) of the knot.

Take the long strips and lay them out in a bunch so that you can easily reach the ends. Poke the end of each strip through the netting of the dress and tie a knot, trimming the excess. Tie the ends of the strips around the circumference of the dress, spacing them as evenly apart as possible.

When you're through, twist the dress again and place the ball on a flat surface, stretching the streamers out behind it.

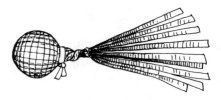

For the finishing touch, take the remaining strip and wrap it from the knot to about two inches (5cm) below where the streamers are tied, hiding the dress. Begin by placing the dress in the middle of the strip and wrapping the two ends around "mummy-fashion" until you have just enough left to make a secure knot.

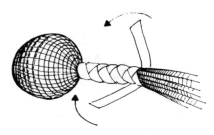

Test your streamer ball for weight and streamer length. If the streamers are too long, trim them. If you'd like a more dramatic streamer effect, you can slice your one-inch (2.5cm) wide streamers lengthwise in halves or thirds.

Now you're ready for the fun.

Throwing a Streamer Ball

The correct way to throw and catch a streamer ball is—guess!—by the streamers. To throw, grasp the streamers two feet (.6m) from where they join the ball. Hold your throwing arm out sideways from your body and your throwing hand parallel to your shoulder. With a circular motion, swing the ball three times around in a "lasso" motion—clockwise, if you're right-handed, and counter-clockwise if you're a lefty—until it builds momentum. As the ball swings forward in its third circle, release your grip and watch it soar skyward, trailing its streamers.

To catch: Avoid the ball and grab for the streamers. It's as easy as that! The best catch is one that nabs the streamers two feet (.6m) from where they join the ball—where the thrower grasps them. The catcher, in a graceful movement, catches the streamers, swings the ball three times around and tosses it back to the thrower.

It's best to toss a streamer high in the air rather than parallel to the ground. Not only does this make for better watching, but it's easier for the catcher if the ball drops down in front of him rather than whizzes by.

If you grasp the streamers at a distance greater than two feet from where they join the ball, the momentum of your throw will be increased, but your throw will be less accurate.

Got it? Now to the games . . .

Streamer Ball Catch

Players:	4–12, but always an even number
Materials:	Streamer ball
Surface:	Paved, grassy or sandy

This noncompetitive game alternates throwing the ball by its streamers with throwing the ball as a ball. Every player gets to do both.

Players form a wide circle, each player standing no less than 10, and no more than 30 yards (.9m–27m) from his neighbor—the fewer the players, the greater the distance between each player.

In a four-player game, the first player *streams* the ball clockwise to the second player who catches it—that is, catches the *ball*—and *throws* it clockwise to the third player, who *streams* it to the fourth player, who *throws* it back to the first player. Now the first player *throws* the ball to the second player who *streams* it to the third, who *throws* it to the fourth, and so on.

When the ball makes four complete revolutions, the game is over.

Twister Stick

Players:	2–6
Materials:	Streamer ball
	Broom handles, sawed off to 3 feet (.9m): 1 for each player
Surface:	Paved, grassy or sandy

In this game, throwing and catching the streamer ball involves unravelling and ravelling the streamers around the broom handle—a challenging feat and one that's recommended only if you've mastered the basic throw and catch techniques. For starters, it's a good idea to have players concentrate either on throwing, or on catching—one player only holding the stick.

The trick of catching a streamer ball "no hands" involves a strong thumb and a quick twist of the wrist as the streamer sails past your stick. Hold the stick firmly and high, four fingers wrapped tightly around the front, thumb pointed up against the back. Allow the streamers to pass close alongside the stick near your thumb until you're ready to snare one. Then, bend your thumb outward and snap it back, pinching a streamer against the stick. Make a circular motion with the stick so that the streamers coil upwards to the top and the ball comes to rest. Your catch is complete.

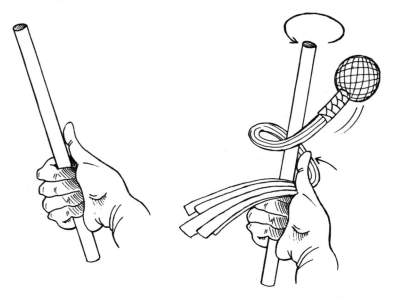

To throw the ball from the stick, reverse the process: Keep your thumb pressed firmly against the streamer while making a circular motion with the stick in the opposite direction. The streamer uncoils and the ball gains momentum. Release your thumb as the ball swings forward in its circle.

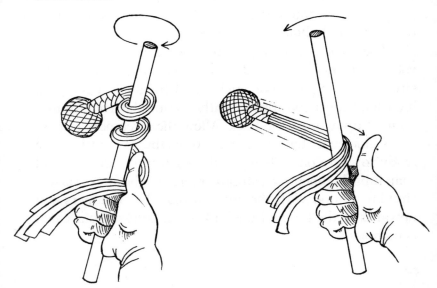

Try a relaxed volley until all players are ready to begin the game.

To play "Twister Stick," players stand in a circle 20 feet (6m) apart. Player #1 begins the game by throwing the ball to Player #2, who throws it to Player #3, and so on around the circle, until someone misses a catch. That player is out of the game. If the throw is poor—hitting the ground short of the distance between players—the thrower gets two more chances before he's out.

The remaining player wins the game.

Snake-by-the-Tail _____

Players: 2 + a referee
Materials: Streamer ball
Surface: Paved, grassy or sandy

This game adheres to standard two-player serving rules: the first player serves to the second player five times, during which time the second player either scores points for himself or misses the catch, scoring a point for the server.

Players #1 and #2 stand at least 15 yards (13.5m) apart. Player #1 serves by streaming the ball to Player #2, who returns it. Player #1 returns the return, and Player #2 makes the catch as far *back* along the streamer as possible—"grabbing the snake by the tail" and holding it. The further back he catches it, the greater the number of points he gets. The referee calls the number of points by measuring the distance in hand-lengths (his) between Player #2's hold and the surface of the ball.

Player #1 repeats the serve for four more rounds, with Player #2 either scoring on the third volley of each round or missing a catch.

After the fifth round, Player #2 serves. A receiving player may only score on the third volley, but any dropped or missed ball counts as a point for the server.

The first player to reach 50 points wins the game. The winner changes places with the referee for the next game.

Through the Roof

Players: 6–10 (2–6 and 4 "helpers")
Materials: Streamer ball for each player
Spoon for each player
Old sheet, the wider the better
Scissors
Surface: Paved, grassy or sandy

Take the old sheet and make several alternating rows of slits, each slit about four inches (10cm) long and each four inches from its nearest neighbor. Make sure the rows aren't placed too close together—the idea is to create a surface in which there are as many places for the ball to drop through as there are places for it to settle.

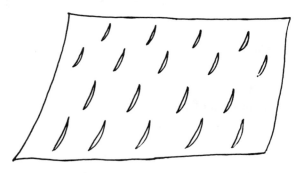

Next, each helper takes a corner and pulls hard, lifting the taut sheet to the height of four feet (1.2m).

Each player takes his streamer ball, bunches the streamers at the midway point, and knots them around the middle of a spoon creating a kind of "anchor."

Players stand 12 yards (10.8m) from the stretched sheet and the game begins.

They take turns throwing their streamer balls high in the air so that they drop onto the sheet. A ball that hits the sheet and remains on top counts for no points; a ball that drops all the way through to hit the ground counts as five points; and a ball that drops halfway through to dangle—its spoon anchor catching in the hole—counts as 10 points.

The first player to reach 50 points wins the game, and the winner usually changes places with one of the "helpers" for the next game.

Box Volleyball

Players:	**2–12 (1–6 on a team)**
Materials:	**3 squares of foam rubber, each 15 inches (37.5cm) square by 5 inches (12.5cm) thick**
	Tube of epoxy glue
	Chalk or tape for marking boundaries
	2 poles, each 7 feet (2.1m) long
	Volleyball net
Surface:	**Grassy or sandy or volleyball court**

Some of the most familiar games take on a whole new dimension with just a small "tweak" in the rules. Such is the case with "Box Volleyball." The box is actually a square "ball" made from three pieces of foam rubber glued together. You can buy odd-sized pieces of foam rubber in many hardware, fabric, or craft supply stores.

Use a thick epoxy glue, also found in most hardware stores, to glue the sections. A ribbon of glue around the edge of each square insures a sturdy bond. Allow your square ball to dry overnight.

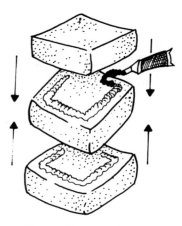

You can play volleyball anywhere. If you don't have a regular volleyball court, you can make one yourself. Draw a court 30 feet (9m) wide for the end lines and 60 feet (18m) long. At the midway point of the long side, drive the poles into the ground at opposite sides of the court. They should stand 6 feet (1.8m) high. String the net across the poles at the same height. Both the dimensions of the court and the height of the net may be adjusted proportionally for younger players.

If there are more than three players on a team, the players stand in two rows so that the front and back areas of the court are covered. Players also rotate clockwise for the serve, which comes from any point behind the end lines.

One of the team captains tosses a coin at the beginning of the match either for first serve or for the side of the court for the first game. The loser of the toss gets the remaining choice.

The player who is serving stands just behind the end line and hits the ball with one open or closed hand so that it flies over the net and lands in the other court. The players on the other court return the ball by using any part of the upper body—hands, chest, shoulder, forearm, and head.

The volley continues until one team drops the ball, scoring a point for the other team; hits the ball out-of-bounds; or catches it in the net. The servers rotate for the next volley, and teams change sides of the court after five points.

The game is played to 11 or 15 points—but to win, a team must have a two-point lead.

Why volleyball with a square ball? Because it's fun!

Throwing Tops

Players: **2–5**
Materials: **Tops, one for each player**
                Chalk for marking game boards
Surface: **Paved**

A very ancient pastime, throwing tops makes for a variety of wonderful games.

Though harder to find nowadays, the best wooden tops have metal tips and stand about 3 inches (7.5cm) tall. Spun by coiling the string around a ribbed edge and throwing the top from the hand, a well-balanced top will knock out the competition!

Several kinds of top games exist, each with a different challenge. One group of games calls for landing your top on a section of a gameboard with the highest point value. Another calls for knocking your competitors' tops down or off the board. A third—and probably the most common group of games—involves throwing tops to see whose spins the longest—the winner receiving a point after each throw.

Some interesting playing designs follow:

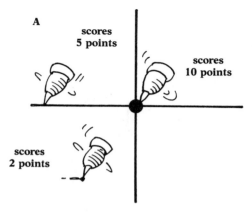

In design A, the player who lands his top at the intersection of the two lines receives 10 points; a top landing on one of the lines receives 5 points; and a top landing anywhere else within the quadrants receives 2 points. Missing the board altogether counts as no points.

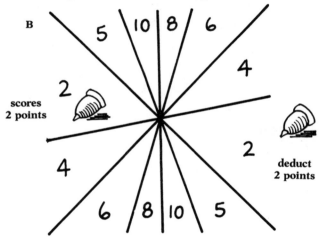

In design B, the playing area consists of a circle divided into unequal segments, numbered for points. Players attempt to get their tops to "die" in the segment with the highest point value. Any player whose top dies beyond the boundaries of the circle deducts, from his or her total, the point value of the nearest segment.

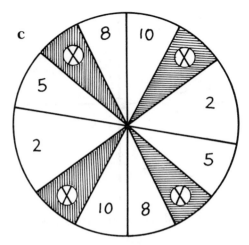

Design C presents possibilities for a sharpshooter. While the first player's top spins, the second player throws his top with the intention of both scoring and knocking the first player into one of the "dead zones," marked by an "X." A player knocked dead three times loses the game.

Throwing tops inspires new ideas for games. Try inventing some! The sky's the limit!

Whip-Ball

Players:	3–11 (1–5 on a team) + a referee
Materials:	3-foot (1m) length of old garden hose
	Spaulding "pink" rubber ball
	Chalk for drawing "home plate"
Surface:	Paved

This abbreviated version of baseball has the added oddity of a flexible bat—don't laugh until you've tried it!

One player, the batter, stands sideways on home plate with arms down, holding the hose with one hand and the ball with the other. When he is ready to bat, he extends his throwing arm and tosses the ball straight up at a distance of about three feet (1m) from his body. He swings the hose wide with his batting arm, connecting with the ball as it descends—*whap!* Unlike a rigid bat, a flexible bat bends backwards during the initial stage of the swing, but whips forward for the later, or connecting, stage. The result can be a ball that sails far and wide!

The players from the other team stand 15 yards (13.5m) from the batter and try to catch the ball before it bounces. One bounce counts as a single for the batter's team; two bounces, a double; three bounces, a triple; and four bounces, a home run. If the ball is caught on the fly by the fielding team, it counts as an automatic *out* and the teams switch sides. The referee tallies runs and keeps an accurate score.

The first team to score 21 points wins the game.

Whirligig

Players:	**5–10**
Materials:	**Long rope (at least 6 feet (1.8m) long)**
	Old shoe or 2 socks tied together and filled with sand
Surface:	**Paved, grassy or sandy**
Preparation:	**Tie the end of the rope to the old shoe or sand-filled socks.**

One player, the Whirligig, stands in the middle of a circle, spinning around and swinging the rope. With the proper amount of weight at the end of it, the rope will swing straight out.

The other players jump over the rope as it sweeps past them, taking care not to trip. The Whirligig may vary both the speed and the height of the rope, gradually lifting it higher and higher until the jumpers realize they must crouch instead of jump for a turn or two. Or, the Whirligig may keep the rope just at the height where nobody is really sure *what* to do—a time when nerves of steel come in handy!

Any jumpers who lose their footing are out of the game. This rule includes the Whirligigs, who have been known, on occasion, to collapse from dizziness. If this happens, the Whirligig chooses one of the jumpers to replace him.

The remaining jumper is the winner.

8
Field, Stream & Sidewalk

It's a beautiful day, and you have a choice to make in your game-playing options—stay in the yard, or explore that wide-open field just behind the grocery store? Organize something that lasts for hours, or just kill a little time before dinner? Scare up about 50 of your closest friends, or just settle for the Snodgrass twins who *never* seem to have anything to do. Whatever—the games in this chapter will give you some ideas.

So whether you choose to camp on Dad's driveway for "London," or pack up your map and compass for "Capture the Flag"—we guarantee a day of great playing!

Capture the Flag _____

Players: 8–20 (4–10 on a team)
Materials: Chalk for marking boundaries
            2 flags (or different colored shirts), one for
            each team
Surface: Paved or grassy

"Capture the Flag" works in either large or small areas. You can play a "tennis court" version with clearly marked boundaries, or stretch the game over hills and fields, schoolyards and front porches. Whatever the scale, the best players use strategy, cunning—and wear running shoes!

The classic version of this game requires each team to have a small flag that it plants firmly in the ground. However, teams may substitute brightly colored shirts for flags—placing them either on the ground, or tying them (not too tightly) to trees, bushes and lampposts.

Divide players into two teams and mark out the "country" for each—a chalk line may divide one country from the other, or a line of trees or lampposts could do it. Mark out a prison on each side also. Each team plants a flag on its own territory that may be either in plain view or hidden—teams agreeing on this beforehand.

Team captains usually devise strategies, dividing their teams into offensive and defensive units: The defenders stay behind to guard their team's flag, while the offenders go behind enemy lines. Acceptable techniques of infiltration include hiding, sneaking, running and rushing *en masse* across the border.

The object: To steal the enemy's flag and bring it safely back to your own country while avoiding capture and imprisonment behind enemy lines. A defender captures an invader by holding him long enough to say "Caught" three times. If the captured player has already managed to nab the enemy flag, then the team captain must decide, based on team strategy, whether to put the flag back in its original position or someplace new. A captured player remains in prison until a teammate runs through his cell shouting "Free!" three times in a row.

The first team to capture the flag and bring it home wins the game.

Drowning Stream _____

Players: **4–10**
Materials: **Rope, or two long sticks for marking the banks**
               of the stream
Surface: **Paved or grassy**

This is a simple broad-jumping contest turned into a game. Position the ropes or sticks about a foot (1m) apart. These become the banks of the "Drowning Stream." Players agree beforehand whether or not to allow running jumps. Each player then takes a turn leaping over "the stream." Eliminate players who do not successfully make the jump and fall into the stream.

After all the players jump, move the sticks or ropes farther apart to widen the banks. Again, any players who fail in their jumps are out.

After each round of jumps widen the banks still farther. The winning player stays out of the stream.

Steal the Bacon

Players: 11–31 (5–15 on a team) + a referee

Materials: An object to represent the "bacon"—hat, shoe, ball, etc.

Chalk or rope for marking boundary lines

Surface: Paved or grassy

This old-time favorite is fun to play anywhere—even in a gym when rain prevents taking recess outside. Both older and younger children can play at the same time.

Draw a rectangular playing area 20 × 40 feet (6m × 12m) and place the "bacon" in the center. Divide the players into two teams. Line up each team behind the narrow edges of the rectangle at opposite sides, 40 feet (12m) apart. Players stand three feet (1m) apart and each team counts off so that every player has a number.

The game begins when the referee, who stands in the middle—but to the side of the playing area—calls out a number. The players from both teams who have the same number dash out to "steal the bacon." The player who carries the bacon back to his team without being tagged by the other player gains a point. If the player with the bacon is tagged, the tagger's team receives a point.

The first team to accumulate 25 points wins the game.

London

Players:	2–6
Materials:	Chalk
	Bottlecaps or checkers for throwing, one for each player
Surface:	Paved

"London," an unusual combination of "Hopscotch" and "Hangman," requires patience, patience, patience. It helps if you're really good friends with the other players!

Draw a rectangle three feet (1m) across by five feet (1.5m) deep and divide it into seven sections. Connect the two corners of the top section with a curved line and write the word "London" in it.

Player #1 stands at the foot of the diagram and throws her bottlecap so that it lands in one of the sections. She draws a small circle (representing a head) in that space, initials it, and throws again. If her bottlecap lands in a different rectangle, she draws another small circle and initials it. If her second or third throw lands in a section she's already initialed, she draws a larger circle (a body) under the smaller one. If the next throw lands in the section with a head and body, she adds a leg, and so on, until she completes a picture of a person. If she lands in the space marked "London," she can then draw one head in every space or add a body or leg to men already started. Each player throws until his or her piece lands on a line between sections or outside the board.

When a player completes one man, she begins a new one next to the first. When she completes three men, she then concentrates on landing her bottlecap in the three-man section again. If she is successful, she draws a line through the three men, adding arms and linking them together. She now "owns" that section. Any player who lands in a section owned by another player loses a turn.

When all the sections are owned, the player with the greatest number of them wins the game.

Poison Pot

Players:	7–12 + a referee
Materials:	Chalk for drawing the poison pot
Surface:	Paved

Just imagine a bubbling pot waiting for its first victim—that's the scary idea behind this wrestling-type game.

Players link arms and form a circle. Inside the circle the referee draws a smaller circle or "poison pot." At the referee's starting signal, players wriggle around and try to force one another into the poison pot. When any player falls or steps into the pot, the referee calls "Out," and the player is out of the game. The circle re-forms, and, at the referee's next starting signal, the struggle resumes.

When too few players remain to form a circle by linking arms, they hold hands and attempt to drag one another into the pot.

The sole surviving player wins.

9
Everybody Wins!

It's not about winning or losing, it's how you play the game, right? Well, if you weren't sure before, the games in this chapter will convince you once and for all. Cooperative games are great for younger players who are often intimidated by the competitive nature of game playing, and they're excellent for "breaking the ice" at a party or picnic where everybody doesn't know anybody. Besides, sometimes you just want to kick back and get silly—maybe you're laughing too hard to count points anyway!

Catch the Ball

Players: 12–20
Materials: Medium-sized inflated ball (or basketball, soccerball)
Surface: Paved or grassy

Players stand in a circle with one player in the center. The players in the circle toss the ball to one another at random, trying to keep it from the center player, who tries to intercept it or knock it from the hands of another player. The ball may be tossed as high or as low, as fast or as lazily as you please, so long as it's out of reach of the center player.

If the center player intercepts or knocks the ball from a circle player, he changes places with the last person to touch the ball. If a circle player drops the ball while throwing or catching, he also changes places with the inside player.

No one wins or loses but the fast pace and unpredictability of this game make it fun.

Human Obstacle Course

Players: 8–20
Materials: None
Surface: Grassy

More of an exercise in fun than a game with strict rules, "Human Obstacle Course" can top off a day of strenuous game playing with some well-earned silliness.

Players become Obstacles or Climbers, and do not have to divide into evenly numbered sides. Obstacle players can work alone or with other Obstacle players to form two- or three-person barriers, and Climbers may help one another across Obstacles.

Obstacles scatter themselves in a rough line over a wide field of play. When a Climber reaches an Obstacle, one of the players in the Obstacle explains the correct way to pass. For instance, an Obstacle might consist of three players standing in a line with their feet spread apart. To pass, a Climber might have to crawl under the first player's legs, around the second player, and under the third player's legs. Each Obstacle comes up with its own requirements for passing and explains them to the Climbers as they arrive.

Climbers & Obstacles

You can make a game of "Human Obstacle Course" by dividing the players into two teams—the Climbers and the Obstacles. The Obstacles try to make as difficult a course as possible for the Climbers. Then, the sides reverse.

Both teams are timed. The team that crosses the obstacle course in a shorter amount of time wins the game.

Human Chairs

Players: 5–10
Materials: None
Surface: Paved or grassy

A cooperative game, "Human Chairs" helps you get to know your neighbor!

Choose a leader to call the steps. Players begin by standing shoulder-to-shoulder in a tight circle. Then, at a signal from the leader, everyone turns to the right, grasps the waist of the person in front, and pulls the circle together even more tightly by moving in towards the center.

Now the tricky part: When the leader shouts "Sit," each player tries to sit on the knees of the person behind him or her, creating one huge "human chair." Of course, everyone will try to accomplish this without falling over!

The leader now takes this human chair, while seated, through a variety of movements such as walking forward, revolving, holding arms out to the side, and so on.

Follow the leader's commands until everyone falls down exhausted, collapsing the circle. Chasing the leader down the street and out of town often follows.

Bump Tag

Players: 10–31
Materials: None
Surface: Paved or grassy

No one wins or loses in "Bump Tag" but it's great for giggles—especially when younger players participate.

Choose one player to be "It" and divide the rest of the players into groups of three. Each group links up in a line by holding waists. The front player is the "Head," the rear player the "Tail."

"It" chases the groups of players and tries to link onto a Tail. If he succeeds, he yells "Bump!" and the head player breaks off and becomes the new "It," while the second player in line becomes the new Head.

The fun in this game involves twisting and turning in order to keep "It" from linking on.

Play until everyone has a chance to be "It."

Foot Beanball

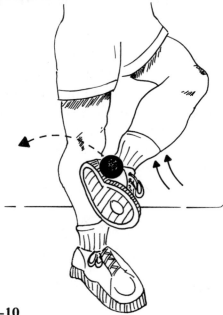

Players:	3–10
Materials:	Beanbag-ball, sold in sports shops; or constructed from an old nylon sock and popcorn kernels.
Surface:	Paved, grassy or sandy

A popular tossing game originating in South America, "Foot Beanball" combines skill and grace in a relaxing, noncompetitive activity. Or, it can be played as an elimination game—a missed catch taking a player out of the game, the last player winning.

To construct a beanball, fill an old nylon sock with two cups of popcorn kernels and sew shut, trimming the excess material. Nylon, or some other thin fabric, "gives" by flattening out slightly when kicked from player to player—an advantage for fancier catches and shots.

Players stand three feet (1m) apart in a circle facing the center. One player starts the volley by balancing the beanball on the inside edge of his right foot before he flips it to the player on his left.

The basic technique of the game involves throwing the ball with the right foot and catching it on the inside edge of the left foot. Since the ball always moves counter-clockwise, you must transfer the ball from your left foot to your right foot to throw it. It takes some practice but is well worth the effort.

You may also toss the ball by using your heels and toes, as well as knees, elbows and wrists. The "rules" discourage using your hands—that would be too easy. You may balance the beanball anywhere else on your body before tossing it. If you drop it, you pick it up with a sideways sweep of the foot—that is, if you're not playing the game for elimination.

Once you get proficient at tossing, you will eventually develop a "juggling" technique—bouncing the ball all over yourself before tossing it to the next player. Great fun!

Back-to-Back Race

Players: 4–20, but always an even number + a referee.
Materials: Chalk or rope for marking start and finish lines
Surface: Paved or grassy

A race between pairs of racers rather than individuals, "Back-to-Back Race" makes both competing *and* cooperating fun.

Draw a start and finish line 10 yards (9m) apart. The pairs of racers sit sideways on the ground behind the starting line, back-to-back, with arms folded across their chests. At the "Go" signal from the referee, they try to stand up together, leaning against each other's backs, without unfolding their arms. Once up, each pair walks to the finish line, still leaning, and attempts to sit down again. If a pair of racers falls while crossing, they lose valuable time since they must get up—arms folded and back-to-back—just as they did at the beginning of the race.

The first pair of racers to rise, cross and sit behind the finish line wins.

Thread the Hoop

Players: 12–30
Materials: 1 or 2 Hula-hoops—if 2, the second should be smaller than the first
Surface: Paved, grassy or sandy

Great for younger players who enjoy crawling through things and getting all tangled up, "Thread the Hoop" is also pure hilarity to watch.

Players stand in a circle holding hands with the Hula-hoop dangling from one player's arm. Players move the hoop around the circle and back to the starting point by stepping through it and sliding it along to the next player—taking care that feet, legs, shoulders or heads don't get caught, tripping you and breaking the circle.

Two Hoop Thread

To play the game with two hoops, find a smaller-sized hoop that can easily pass through the first hoop. Begin with the hoops at opposite sides of the circle. Pass them towards each other as before, and one through the other where they meet. This will require some fancy footwork for one of the players. However, if you pass around the hoops at various speeds, the problem passes to someone different each time around.

Hoop Racing

To make the game into a race, you need at least 20 players forming two circles and two Hula hoops of the same size. The first circle to pass the hoop back to the starting player wins the race.

Odd Ball

Players: 12–20
Materials: Medium-sized inflated ball (or soccerball, basketball, etc.)
Surface: Paved or grassy

Players form a circle, except for "It" who stands in the middle. Circle players stand with the right foot of each player on the left foot of the neighboring player, which anchors each one in place. Their feet are spread as far apart as is comfortably possible.

"It" gets the ball and attempts to throw or kick it out of the circle between the players' legs. Players try to stop the ball by using arms and legs *only*, and may not change the position of their feet. A circle player who loses his balance while trying to stop the ball changes places with "It."

If "It" manages to throw or kick the ball outside the circle, he changes places with the player between whose legs the ball passed. If the ball escapes by passing *between* two adjacent players, "It" changes places with the player to the right.

Odd One Out

You can reverse this game by having the circle players stand facing outward while "It" (outside the circle this time) attempts to pass the ball inside the circle.

Octopus Tag

Players:	**8–20**
Materials:	**Chalk or rope for marking boundaries**
Surface:	**Paved or grassy**

Wear old clothes for this one—the good-natured rough-housing of "Octopus Tag" can be tough on that new pair of pants or fancy shirt.

Select an Octopus from the players. He or she stands in the center between two boundary lines, drawn 40 feet (12m) apart. The other players stand safely behind either of the boundary lines and wait for the "Go" command from the Octopus, beginning the first round.

At the command, players run across to the opposite side, avoiding the Octopus, who tries to tag them. A tagged player links hands with the Octopus in the next round—becoming a tentacle—and helps to tag additional players. The original Octopus player gives the "Go" command each time.

Assembling the growing Octopus is half the fun of this game. After it has a tentacle, the original Octopus stands still and lets his tentacle do the tagging for him. The tentacle player may stretch out or circle around the original Octopus to tag a runner, but if he or she is dragged away from that stationary position, the runners call "Foul" and the round begins again.

As new runners are tagged, longer and longer tentacles are created with which to tag remaining runners. Tagged runners become part of the Octopus in the next round. The original Octopus holds fast to the tagged player's belt or shirt. This captured runner now has two free hands, either of which may be used to tag the remaining players. This, in addition to the free hand of the original octopus, makes for a three-handed—or three-tentacled—tagging error!

And so the monster grows, until the last runner doesn't stand a chance!

Age Range Chart & Index

Game	Page	Ages			
		6–8	9–12	13–18	Adult
Around the World	77			★	★
Back-to-Back Race	121		★	★	★
Balloon-Face Relay	29	★	★	★	★
Bangball	62		★	★	★
Beach Ball Relay	38			★	★
Bombers	44	★	★	★	★
Boomerang Frisbee	16			★	★
Bottleball	87	★	★	★	★
Bounce-Off Bowling	81	★	★	★	★
Box Volleyball	100			★	★
Bump Tag	119	★	★	★	★
Capture the Flag	108			★	★
Catch the Ball	116	★	★	★	★
Chain Gang Race	36			★	★
Chariot Race	37		★	★	★
Circle Ball Race	61	★	★	★	★
Circle Dodge Ball	63	★	★	★	★
Circle Frisbee	17		★	★	★
Climbers & Obstacles	118	★	★	★	★
Clothespin Handshake	35		★	★	★
Cornerball	55			★	★
Courtsbee	15			★	★
Dizzy Race	28	★	★	★	★
Double Disc Frisbee	13			★	★
Drowning Stream	110	★	★	★	★
Flamingos	86	★	★	★	★
Foot Beanball	120			★	★
Frisbee Bowling	20		★	★	★
Garontki	80			★	★
Goal Line Frisbee	12		★	★	★
Greedy	78			★	★

Age Range Chart & Index

Game	Page	Ages 6–8	Ages 9–12	Ages 13–18	Adult
Greek Ball Game	54			★	★
Guts	10			★	★
Haley-Over or Wall-Ball	58		★	★	★
Half-Ball Baseball	74			★	★
Half-Ball Bowling	84			★	★
Highball	57		★	★	★
Hoop Racing	123		★	★	★
Horse	69			★	★
Human Chairs	118		★	★	★
Human Obstacle Course	117	★	★	★	★
Interferers	34		★	★	★
Junk Shop Relay	31		★	★	★
Kickball	75	★	★	★	★
Lapkta	72			★	★
London	112		★	★	★
Losing Your Marbles	49	★	★	★	★
Milkie	46		★	★	★
Octopus Tag	124	★	★	★	★
Odd Ball	123		★	★	★
Odd One Out	124		★	★	★
Pass the Ball	60		★	★	★
Pass the Grapefruit	27		★	★	★
Peggyball	68			★	★
Piggyback Ball	59			★	★
Pima Relay Race	39			★	★
Poison	50		★	★	★
Poison Pot	113		★	★	★
Potty	49		★	★	★
Punchball	65		★	★	★
Ringer	47		★	★	★
Roll-Ball	88	★	★	★	★

Age Range Chart & Index

Game	Page	Ages 6–8	9–12	13–18	Adult
Save the Fortress	82		★	★	★
Siamese Twins Relay	32	★	★	★	★
Sleeping Bag Relay	24		★	★	★
Snake-by-the-Tail	96			★	★
"Spauldeen" Tennis	64			★	★
Spud	66		★	★	★
Steal the Bacon	111	★	★	★	★
Streamer Ball	90			★	★
Streamer Ball Catch	94			★	★
Street Frisbee	18			★	★
String of Beads	45		★	★	★
Tee Ball	70	★	★	★	★
Thread the Hoop	122		★	★	★
Three-Legged Relay	33		★	★	★
Through the Roof	98			★	★
Throwing Tops	102		★	★	★
Twister Stick	94			★	★
Two Hoop Thread	123		★	★	★
Ultimate Frisbee	21		★	★	★
Whip-Ball	104			★	★
Whirligig	105		★	★	★
Whose Shoes?	26	★	★	★	★
Wiggle Relay	25	★	★	★	★